The Unofficial Ducks Football Trivia, Puzzles & History Book

Dale Ratermann

BLUE RIVER PRESS

Blue River Press
Indianapolis, Indiana

ISBN-13: 9781935628040

Cover Design: Phil Velikan
Cover Photo: John Tutrone, Amazing Moments Photography
Layout: MaryKay Hruskocy Scott
Illustrations: Robert Jackson
Proofread By: MaryKay Hruskocy Scott

Printed in the United States of America
10 9 8 7 6 5 4 3 2 1

Blue River Press
Distributed by Cardinal Publishers Group
Tom Doherty Company, Inc.
www.cardinalpub.com

Table of Contents

Short Yardage Crossword

Solution on page 131.

Across

1. Ducks QB who was the 1983 Pro Bowl MVP
6. Shake up the ball carrier with a hard tackle
9. Map within a map
10. One of the football officials, briefly
11. Poke fun at a teammate
12. Faint lighting in the stadium
13. Send a Twitter note from the stands
15. Treatment for a player's sprained ankle
17. Month for Pac-10 Track & Field Championships
18. West Indies native
20. Oregon state tree: Douglas ___
21. Scrunch
25. UN workers' grp.
26. Out and away (2 wds.)
27. UO basketball practice site
28. Ducks All-American RB in 1971

Down

1. In shape
2. Four quarters?
3. Olympics chant
4. *Consumer Reports* employee
5. Chez Ray's North Beach cioppino seafood dish
6. Southern Israel in the Bible
7. Fictional island in *Jaws*
8. Engine speed, for short
14. Fertilized egg
15. In a cold manner
16. Bounce off a would-be tackler
19. Part of a nuclear arsenal, briefly
20. Mediterranean fruit
22. ET's craft
23. Scratch the surface of
24. Opposite of post-

After solving the crossword puzzle, use the letters in the grid to answer the additional clue. Transfer the letters in numbered boxes to the corresponding blanks below. (Or answer the additional clue first to help you solve the crossword puzzle.)

Ducks bowl game on Jan. 1, 2002 vs. Colorado

___ ___ ___ ___ ___ ___
1   19   14   5   13   7

Chapter 1

History

The first football team was formed at the University of Oregon in 1893, and played its first game in 1894. Oregon beat Albany College, 44-2, in the initial contest and finished the season with a 1-2-1 record.

Oregon played in the Rose Bowl following the 1916 season and beat Penn, 14-0. UO got back to the Rose Bowl after the 1919 season, losing to Harvard, 7-6. Oregon didn't return to postseason play until the 1949 Cotton Bowl when the Ducks lost to Southern Methodist, 21-13. From 1989 through 2011, Oregon played in 18 bowl games in 22 years.

The Ducks' first appearance at No. 1 in the national polls occurred on Oct. 17, 2010. Oregon lost to Auburn, 22-19, in the 2011 BCS National Championship Game.

The annual Oregon-Oregon State University game is known as The Civil War. The series began in 1894 and is the seventh oldest rivalry game in the nation. Oregon currently leads the series, 58-46-10. Oregon also has a heated rivalry with the University of Washington. The schools first played in 1910.

Among the greatest players in Oregon history are quarterbacks Norm Van Brocklin, Dan Fouts, George Shaw, Bob Berry, Akili Smith and Joey Harrington; defensive backs Mel Renfro, Herman O'Berry, Chris Oldham, Jairus Byrd, Chad Cota and Alex Molden; receivers Ahmad Rashad (a.k.a. Bobby Moore) and Lew Barnes; tight end Russ Francis; defensive linemen Nick Reed, Vince Goldsmith, Haloti Ngata and George Martin; offensive linemen Gary Zimmerman, Adam Snyder, Tom Drougas, Steve Barnett and Fred Quillan; linebacker Dave Wilcox; and running backs Tuffy Leemans, Derek Loville, Jonathan Stewart, Reuben Droughns and LaMichael James.

History Crossword
Solution on page 131

Across

1. Had popcorn at an Autzen Stadium concession stand
4. 1994 All-American safety who had an 8-year NFL career
8. Exhales audibly
13. Ducks wrestler's goal
14. UO faculty member, briefly
15. Once a year, like the Ducks spring football game
16. Bon Jovi lyrics: "No one said that ___ be easy . . . "
17. FieldTurf layer's calculation
18. 1962-63 All-American HB who was a 10-time Pro Bowl selection as a Cowboys DB
19. Training room balm ingredient
21. Angry display for a ref's call
23. Super Bowl mo.
24. 1970 All-American QB who played four NFL seasons as a Saints WR
28. Hurting, following a tough practice
30. Cargo
32. Incite the crowd
36. One of the five Ws from a pressbox reporter
39. Declare your team loyalty
40. Like an Autzen Stadium suite seat
41. Charged particle
42. Surround
45. Poetry class "before"
46. Joe Paterno's eyeglasses, for short
48. Organic compound from Chemistry 101
49. Hide-hair connector
50. Chapala Mexican Restaurant coin

51. PK Park diamond
54. Prefix with legal or graph
56. 1971 All-American OT who was a 1st round pick of the Colts
60. Sakura Japanese Restaurant sash
63. 2004 and '05 Joe Schaffeld Award winner, Devan ___
65. Prying
66. 1995 All-American CB who played 8 NFL seasons with the Saints, Chargers and Lions
68. Type of pass patterns
72. Half a sawbuck
73. Stupidity
74. Curved molding
75. Stadium brouhaha
76. Offensive, defensive and special
77. 1954 All-American QB replaced in the NFL by Johnny Unitas
78. University of Arizona color

Down

1. Pertaining to bees
2. Pac-10 championship
3. Fund a UO scholarship
4. University bean counter, for short
5. Boston Bruins legend, Bobby ___
6. Foot injury: Turf ___
7. Way, way off, like the University of Hawaii
8. Show of contempt to an OSU fan
9. Campus Cottage B&B ___
10. Malarkey
11. Tortoise racer
12. Messy student dresser
15. Team's specialized vocabulary
20. Santa's little helper
22. Ducks baseball bat wood
25. Middle Easterners
26. *Scream* star Campbell

27. Fizzles out
29. Swelled head for an All-American, maybe
31. Charlie Brown: "Good ___!"
33. Black cat, to some
34. Player's bushy do
35. Textile worker
36. Bit of smoke
37. Eugene's New ___ Christian College
38. Change for a five at Chase Bank
40. Oregon Symphony stringed instrument
43. Home of Phillips University
44. Game attendee
47. Stadium security guard, often
51. Sarcasm
52. One of the Bobbsey twins
53. UO equestrian team horse color
55. Smart guys?
57. Succeed following graduation (2 wds.)
58. Line to an Encore Theatre audience
59. Church council
60. Leave off the Ducks roster
61. Olympic skier, ___ Miller
62. Pelvic bones
64. Sticky substances
67. Joe DiMaggio's brother
69. "Yuck!"
70. Alternative drink at Starbucks
71. Repair a uniform tear

Duck Soup

Find items in the categories listed, going up, down, sideways or diagonally in the letter grid on the next page. No letter is used more than once. When you have found all 21 items, there should be 40 unused letters. Starting at the top of the grid, moving from left to right, and working down, fill in the spaces below the grid with those unused letters to spell out a hidden phrase. Hint: The phrase is part of a song's lyrics. (Bonus points if you know the song's title.) Solution on page 132.

6 UO Football All-Americans

_____

_____

_____

_____

_____

_____

5 Players on 2010 UO Team

_____

_____

_____

_____

_____

4 Former UO Coaches

_____

_____

_____

_____

3 UO Bowl Games

_____

_____

_____

2 UO Colors

_____

_____

1 UO Athletics Director

_____

```
                  D
               O  R  E
            E  G  O  N  E
         S  A  M  O  H  T  R
      I  T  T  O  L  L  E  B  O
   U  R  A  L  M  A  T  S  E  I  F
A  M  A  T  E  R  W  D  A  E  R  E  O
A  N  I  L  K  C  O  R  B  N  A  V  R
W  V  I  M  G  L  H  L  M  S  W  S  F
B  G  O  R  O  A  U  N  A  K  O  E  N
A  E  E  N  R  O  E  R  T  O  L  M  E
R  E  A  R  A  D  R  D  T  O  L  A  R
N  O  I  R  L  S  T  E  H  R  E  J  S
   S  S  O  D  A  A  H  E  B  Y  N
      M  E  E  T  E  C  W  O  E
         S  N  O  A  N  S  L
            U  C  D  O  L
               N  N  U
                  M
```

Hidden Phrase:

— — — — — —, — — — — — — —

— — — — —, — — — — — —

— — — — — — — — — — —

— — — — —.

Bowl Game Categories

For each of the categories listed, come up with a name, word or phrase beginning with each letter of the words BOWL GAME. Our solution on page 132.

	Former UO Defensive Player	Former UO Offensive Player
B		
O		
W		
L		
G		
A		
M		
E		

	Football Term	Oregon City
B		
O		
W		
L		
G		
A		
M		
E		

Wilcox Sudoku

Use logic to fill in the boxes so every row, column and 2 x 3 box contains the letters W-I-L-C-O-X, in honor of former UO star Dave Wilcox. The two-way star (guard on offense and end on defense) played for the Ducks in 1962-63, then went on to an 11-year career in the NFL with the San Francisco 49ers as a linebacker. He was elected to the Pro Football Hall of Fame in 2000. Solution on page 131.

		W			L
		X		O	
W			X		C
X		I			O
	X		O		
I			L		

Who Am I? Sudoku

Use logic to fill in the boxes so every row, column and 3 x 3 box contains the letters of the name of a memorable Oregon player. (Hint: He was a two-way star who won an NFL championship and earned all-pro honors.) When completed, the row indicated by the arrow will spell out the name correctly. Solution on page 133.

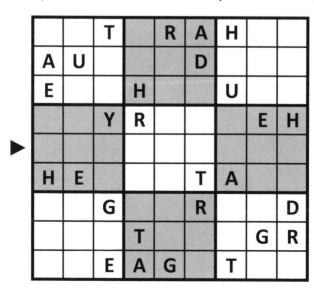

Bobby Moore

Oregon History Trivia
Answers on page 132.

1. Which Ducks' two-way star led the nation with 10 interceptions in 1945, then led the Pacific Coast Conference in rushing and scoring in 1947?

2. Who were the brothers that led Oregon to the 1917 Rose Bowl?

3. In late 2009, KVAL-TV named the top 10 UO players of the 2000s. Who was No. 1?

4. Is the Ducks' record for most total yards in a game (vs. New Mexico in 2010) more or less than 700 yards?

5. Oregon scored 115 points vs. Puget Sound in 1910. The team's modern day record is 72 points, set in 1999 and matched in 2010. Who were those games against?

6. What is the UO record for most points in a Civil War game? Hint: It happened in 2008.

7. The Ducks set a school record with 12 consecutive wins in 2010. That broke the mark of 11 set when?

8. When was the last time UO had a losing season?

9. When was the first time the Ducks won 10 games in a season?

10. When the Ducks won the Pac-10 title in 1994, when was their previous conference championship?

11. Who were the four co-captains of the 2009 team?

12. When was the last time UO played Notre Dame?

13. Which school has Oregon beaten the most in its history?

14. When was the first time UO appeared in the Top 10 of the Associated Press poll?

15. In 1971, Oregon and Washington State played some place other than Eugene or Pullman. Where was that game played?

16. When was the first season the Ducks played in Autzen Stadium?

17. Where did UO play before Autzen Stadium?

18. Which UO quarterback had 500 yards of total offense in a Fiesta Bowl?

19. Who set the UO bowl game record with three QB sacks vs. Ohio State in the Rose Bowl on Jan. 1, 2010?

20. Which school did the Ducks beat in the 1963 Sun Bowl for UO's first bowl win since the 1917 Rose Bowl?

21. Who did Oregon play its first overtime game against (in 1996)?

22. From 1999-2010, the Ducks were 5-1 in overtime games. Who was the loss against?

23. Which Ducks halfback was tackled by Washington fans in 1962 while he tried to catch a game-winning touchdown pass?

24. Name two of the four members of the 1963 UO backfield known as "The Firehouse Four."

25. When did Oregon begin the Homecoming football game tradition: 1926, 1936 or 1946?

Short Yardage Crossword

Solution on page 134.

Across

1. Ducks DE who led the Pac-10 in QB sacks in 2009
5. Singing syllables
8. Olympic fencer
10. Molala Indian pole
11. Cow or sow at the Oregon State Fair
12. CD World section
14. Disobeyed an Oregon Zoo sign?
17. High-fives on the sidelines
20. Toward a player's face
22. Canadian island near Newfoundland
23. Ducks OG who was a Pac-10 Academic All-Conference pick

Down

1. Less common
2. A great European painter (2 wds.)
3. Used to be
4. UO campus shade trees
5. Dontae Williams' uniform number
6. Decompose
7. Training room backrub response
8. Sore the morning after a game
9. Gossipy about the Ducks
13. Ship board
15. Unit of work
16. Small boat
18. Everyone on the team
19. Thickness
21. *The Matrix* hero

After solving the crossword puzzle, use the letters in the grid to answer the additional clue. Transfer the letters in numbered boxes to the corresponding blanks below. (Or answer the additional clue first to help you solve the crossword puzzle.)

Offensive lineman who spent two years in Spain on a religious mission before enrolling at UO in 2007

___ ___ ___ ___ ___
18 11 13 4 1

Chapter 2

Championship Game Team

It was a matchup of No. 1 vs. No. 2—two undefeated teams. And in the end, it was Auburn beating Oregon, 22-19, on a last-second field goal at Glendale's University of Phoenix Stadium.

The game was seen by 27.3 million people on ESPN, making it the highest rated cable TV program in history.

The Ducks earned a spot in the title game by going 12-0 in the 2010 regular season, the most memorable in Oregon history. The Ducks led the nation in scoring (46.8 points per game) and total offense (530 yards per game).

Oregon's high powered offense was led by running back LaMichael James, who was tops in the nation with 1,731 rushing yards, and finished third in the Heisman Trophy voting. Quarterback Darron Thomas threw for 2,881 yards and ran for 486. Jeff Maehl led the team with 77 receptions for 1,076 yards.

Defensively, Oregon led the Pac-10 Conference in rushing defense. Casey Matthews led the team in tackles; Cliff Harris had six interceptions; Kenny Rowe had seven sacks.

Oregon was the first Pac-10 squad to go 9-0 in conference play, beating every other league team. The Ducks added wins against New Mexico, Tennessee and Portland State.

Oregon's head coach, Chip Kelly, was named the National Coach of the Year. Other Ducks who received national honors were James (consensus All-American) and Harris (All-American punt returner). Seven Ducks were named first-team all-Pac-10: RB James, WR Maehl, TE David Paulson, OL Jordan Holmes, LB Matthews, DB Talmadge Jackson and PR Harris. Six other Ducks were named second-team all-Pac-10: QB Thomas, OL Bo Thran, DL Brandon Bair, DL Rowe, DB Harris and ST Bryson Littlejohn. Kelly was named the Pac-10 Coach of the Year.

All Mixed Up

Unscramble the last names of these players on Oregon's 2010 squad. Answers on page 134.

OFFENSE

1. ALNOPSU   _____

2. AHNRT   _____

3. AEIKRS   _____

4. AHMOST   _____

5. AEJMS   _____

6. EIINTU   _____

7. KORY   _____

8. AEPRS   _____

9. ALNOST   _____

10. EEMSW   _____

DEFENSE

1. BEOTTY   _____

2. AEHMSTTW   _____

3. DGILNO   _____

4. ADDKU   _____

5. ACKLR   _____

6. ENRRTU   _____

7. HJNNOOS   _____

8. AEPPPRS   _____

9. AHIRRS   _____

10. EHIJLLNOTT   _____

2010 Top 25 Teams Word Search

Answers on page 135.

```
X  I  R  U  O  S  S  I  M  N  E  V  A  D  A
O  R  E  G  O  N  W  T  I  A  E  V  K  N  L
L  U  M  Z  K  H  Z  S  C  N  T  I  S  I  A
A  G  I  F  L  D  I  A  H  I  E  R  A  S  B
R  U  S  L  A  N  Q  N  I  L  T  G  R  N  A
K  I  S  O  H  A  L  I  G  O  A  I  B  O  M
A  D  I  R  O  L  F  L  A  R  T  N  E  C  A
N  H  S  I  M  Y  D  O  N  A  S  I  N  S  U
S  U  S  D  A  R  R  R  S  C  O  A  W  I  B
A  H  I  A  S  A  O  A  T  H  I  T  U  W  U
S  G  P  S  T  M  F  C  A  T  H  E  Q  B  R
L  W  P  T  A  N  N  T  U  O  C  D  N  N
U  H  I  A  T  I  A  J  E  O  F  H  I  N  K
T  C  S  T  E  E  T  A  T  S  E  S  I  O  B
F  Y  T  E  X  A  S  A  &  M  U  X  J  R  T
```

ALABAMA	MICHIGAN STATE	OREGON
ARKANSAS	MISSISSIPPI ST	SOUTH CAROLINA
AUBURN	MISSOURI	STANFORD
BOISE STATE	N CAROLINA ST	TCU
CENTRAL FLORIDA	NEBRASKA	TEXAS A&M
FLORIDA STATE	NEVADA	TULSA
LSU	OHIO STATE	VIRGINIA TECH
MARYLAND	OKLAHOMA	WISCONSIN
	OKLAHOMA STATE	

2010 Team Crossword
Solution on page 134.

Across

1. Ducks' leading rusher
6. Long-eared beast
9. Left one's seat at the game
14. Set straight
15. UO weight room unit
16. "You ___ believe!"
17. Old-fashioned, like uniforms
18. Spring football mo.
19. Change a pass route
20. Preseason prognosticator, maybe
21. Lose footing on the FieldTurf
23. Distressed cry
24. Pig's digs
26. Sound of astonishment
28. Extra point kicks catchers
31. Stable staple
34. All-Pac-10 QB
38. "___ we there yet?"
39. Bach's musical composition
41. Dress cut
42. On The Rocks choir voice
44. Not even
45. No. 1 hit for Mr. Mister
46. Aquatic mammal at the Oregon Zoo
47. Divine
49. Sixth sense, for short
50. Safety who wore No. 20
52. Albertsons bread choice
53. Middle of March
54. Like Easter eggs
56. Have the cheese bread at Oregon Electric Station
58. Hang out at Gateway Mall
61. Art history class subject
64. Oregon statutes
67. Bay window
69. Silent assent
70. Ducks 1998 bowl game
72. Discontinue
73. Minor player
74. Oregon State, to Oregon
75. Merry-go-round figure, to a child
76. Paulann Petersen's "before"
77. Ducks' leading receiver

Down

1. Pickle container
2. Bier Stein pints
3. Small amount
4. Exit Autzen Stadium
5. Sound of contempt for the refs
6. Quarterbacks' strengths
7. Navy commando
8. Bit of parsley at Keystone Cafe
9. Turkish title
10. Description of an out of shape lineman (2 wds.)
11. Ducks kicker in 1984-85, Dean ___
12. Go Fish Restaurant one-dish meal
13. Ducks QB in 1949-50, ___ Stelle
22. Kick worth one on the scoreboard: Abbr.
25. UO campus map notation: "___ Are Here"
27. Questionable
28. Wealthy one
29. Muse of poetry
30. Short-tempered, like a tired ref
32. All excited at seeing the Ducks
33. English dynasty

35. Bogged down
36. Licorice-like flavor
37. Oozes
39. Blake Thompson's uniform number
40. Small whirlpool
43. Like some of the grapes at Market of Choice
48. Ducks all-time basketball scoring leader, Ron ___
51. Pacific-___ Conference
53. Roma's country
55. Numbskull
57. Dorm room sleep spoiler
58. ___ Ness monster
59. Black-and-white cookie at Safeway
60. Tall tale teller
62. It's in a jamb
63. Halftime lead, e.g.
65. Zigged and zagged through the defense
66. Bygone royal
68. ESPN sportscaster, Bob ___
71. Apiece, in scores

2010 Season Trivia

Answers on page 135.

1. LaMichael James finished third in the Heisman Trophy voting. Who finished ahead of him?

2. Oregon was sixth in the nation with 21 interceptions. Who led the Ducks with six interceptions?

3. Who led the team in scoring?

4. What was the slogan on the 2010 Spirit Tee?

5. Which two Oregon linebackers tied for the Pac-10 lead with three fumble recoveries?

6. Which two Ducks earned All-Pac-10 and Pac-10 All-Academic honors in 2010?

7. The entering freshman class of 2007 set a school record with 41 wins in their four-year careers. Which freshman class previously held the record with 38 wins over a four-year period?

8. Five Oregon players concluded their eligibility in 2010 and played 52 games in their careers, tying the school record held by Ed Dickson. Name three of those players.

9. Oregon set a school record with 528 rushing yards in one game. Which team did the Ducks set the record against?

10. Against which team did LaMichael James rush for his season high?

11. Jeff Maehl had 1,076 pass receiving yards in 2010. Who was the last Oregon player with 1,000+ receiving yards in a season?

12. The Ducks' longest play from scrimmage in 2010 was an 85-yard rush against Arizona. Who had that run?

13. Oregon recorded two shutouts during the 2010 season, the first time the Ducks had multiple shutouts in a season since 1964. Which two teams did the Ducks hold scoreless?

14. Which Ducks running back tied the school's modern day scoring record with five touchdowns in one game?

15. Which Oregon special teams player tied a Pac-10 season record with four punt returns for touchdowns in 2010?

16. The Ducks set a state record for largest attendance at a football game with 60,017. Who was Oregon's opponent for that game in Autzen Stadium?

Casey Matthews

17. In Oregon's season opener against New Mexico, only one player on offense and two on defense were making the first start of their college careers. Who were those three players?

18. Who led the Ducks with 79 total tackles?

19. Who led the Ducks with seven sacks?

20. Besides Jackson Rice, who was the only other player to punt for the Ducks?

21. Who was the only Oregon player to score on a rushing play, pass reception and return?

22. Not counting the team's special BCS Championship Game uniform or the throw-back uniform, the Ducks had four different helmets, five jerseys, four pairs of pants, four sets of socks and four pairs of shoes. How many different possible combinations of uniforms did that create for the Ducks?

23. Which two universities on the Ducks' 2010 schedule did Oregon play for the first time in school history?

24. Who was the Ducks' offensive coordinator?

25. Name two of the four players on the 2010 roster who attended Eugene high schools.

Alston Sudoku

Use logic to fill in the boxes so every row, column and 2 x 3 box contains the letters A-L-S-T-O-N, in honor of Ducks running back Remene Alston. As an added twist, the shaded areas also will contain the letters A-L-S-T-O-N. Solution on page 134.

	A				
		S	T		
		A	L		S
N		L	O		
		T	N		
				O	

Golpashin Sudoku

Use logic to fill in the grid below so that every row, column and 3 x 3 box contains the letters G-O-L-P-A-S-H-I-N, in honor of Ramsen Golpashin, the backup right guard. Solution on page 135.

A			S		H			P
		I				G		
P	N						O	S
		P		O		A		
	H		L		N		S	
		S		A		H		
I	O						N	A
		L				I		
S			I		O			L

(Phil) Knight Moves, Part I

On a standard 8 x 8 chessboard, move from square to square the way a knight moves (between opposite corners of a 2 x 3 rectangle) to spell the last names of the Ducks' 2010 Opening Day offensive starters. (The list of starters is below.) Begin anywhere on the board and place an A (for ASPER) in that square. Now move like a knight and place an S where you land. From there, move like a knight again and place a P in that square, and so on, until you spell out ASPER. From the point where you end ASPER, continue to move like a knight and spell BARNER and the rest of the 11 starters. Here's the tough part: Do not use any square more than once. There are 61 letters in the starters' names, so you have three extra squares on the board to play with. If you get stumped, turn the page for an easier version of the same game.

Starters:

ASPER

BARNER

DAVIS

HOLMES

KAISER

MAEHL

PAULSON

THOMAS

THRAN

TUINEI

YORK

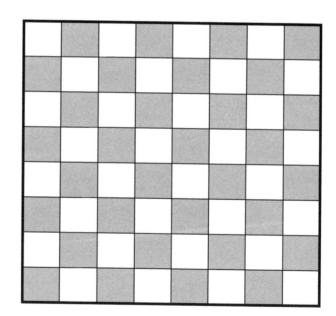

(Phil) Knight Moves, Part II

If you were not able to complete the Part I challenge, one possible solution is below. But where do you start and where do you move? That's the challenge of this puzzle. To begin, go to each A (for ASPER) in the grid and see which go to an S when you move like a knight. There are several possibilities, so from each of the Ss, see if you can move like a knight to get to one of the two Ps on the board. Once you get started, continue to move like a knight to complete ASPER, then move on to BARNER and so on, until you complete the starting lineup. Remember, do not use any square more than once. Solution is on page 136.

Starters:

ASPER

BARNER

DAVIS

HOLMES

KAISER

MAEHL

PAULSON

THOMAS

THRAN

TUINEI

YORK

O	O	A	A	H	I	S	*
N	S	H	R	E	*	T	V
Y	L	E	R	S	K	*	A
P	T	I	M	K	S	A	A
P	R	N	U	U	I	M	R
O	E	A	R	T	D	M	S
B	L	I	L	R	E	E	O
N	S	A	H	N	H	E	A

2010 Season Word Search

Answers on page 137.

```
R  W  B  G  L  E  W  I  S  O  N  H  F  R  P
E  I  R  E  M  L  A  P  W  N  H  N  J  S  E
P  S  M  A  I  L  L  I  W  G  O  U  M  C  B
S  R  A  P  P  E  P  K  S  C  J  E  I  O  E
A  S  L  P  A  Y  S  I  N  G  E  R  Y  Y  A
M  B  I  S  L  T  R  I  P  W  L  E  W  O  R
O  J  A  V  G  R  T  L  X  C  T  A  K  R  D
H  N  O  H  A  S  W  E  H  T  T  A  M  K  S
T  U  O  H  E  D  T  K  R  L  I  B  W  V  H
H  U  K  S  N  J  Y  N  O  S  L  U  A  P  Z
R  D  R  J  K  S  O  K  E  N  O  D  L  I  G
A  D  A  N  A  C  O  R  T  U  I  N  E  I  R
N  A  L  L  E  M  A  N  D  J  G  S  Q  X  E
V  K  C  O  B  R  E  J  M  A  E  H  L  E  J
J  V  H  O  L  M  E  S  W  M  N  E  D  F  T
```

ASPER	JACKSON	LOKOMBO	RICE
BAIR	JAMES	MAEHL	ROWE
BEARD	JOHNSON	MATTHEWS	THOMAS
BOYETT	JORDAN	PALMER	THRAN
CLARK	KADDU	PATTERSON	TUINEI
DAVIS	KAISER	PAULSON	TURNER
GILDON	KELIIKIPI	PAYSINGER	WEEMS
HARRIS	LEWIS	PEPPARS	WILLIAMS
HOLMES	LITTLEJOHN	PLEASANT	YORK

Short Yardage Crossword

Solution on page 137.

Across

1. Popular cooking spray
4. UO fraternity letter
7. Central points
8. Same old, same old
9. Distinctive flair
10. Kampus Barber Shop request
12. Poet T.S. ____
14. Genetic inits.
15. UO book collections
17. Opposite of WSW
18. Computer shortcut
19. Football field increment
21. Canaanite deity
22. Attempt a kick
23. Not pro?
24. Ducks batter's asset
25. Kicker's prop

Down

1. Fertilize like a bee
2. Healthy South American fruit in smoothies (2 wds.)
3. Bush-league
4. Computer monitor, for short
5. U. of Miami athlete
6. Move around
7. Ducks QB known as A.J.
11. Ducks QB who appeared on the cover of *Sports Illustrated* in 2009
13. Scottish cap
16. Morocco's capital
20. Turn green, perhaps

After solving the crossword puzzle, use the letters in the grid to answer the additional clue. Transfer the letters in numbered boxes to the corresponding blanks below. (Or answer the additional clue first to help you solve the crossword puzzle.)

Former Ducks QB who played in Super Bowls VIII, IX and XI

___ ___ ___ ___ ___
21 12 16   8 19

Chapter 3

Quarterbacks

The University of Oregon has been blessed with standout quarterbacks throughout its history.

The first great Oregon quarterback was Charles A. "Shy" Huntington. The All-American led UO to the 1917 Rose Bowl championship and was named to *The Register-Guard*'s all-time Oregon team.

Other All-American quarterbacks include Norm Van Brocklin (1948), George Shaw (1954) and Bob Berry (1964).

Additional first-team all-conference QBs were Bill Steers (1917), Hal Chapman (1923), Dave Grosz (1960 All-Coast), Dan Fouts (1972), Chris Miller (1985-86), Bill Musgrave (1990), Danny O'Neil (1994), Akili Smith (1998), Joey Harrington (2001) and Dennis Dixon (2007).

Statistically, the best ever may turn out to be the Ducks' current signal caller, Darron Thomas. In 2010, the redshirt sophomore led Oregon to a 12-1 record while completing 61.5 percent of his passes for 2,881 yards. He had 30 touchdown passes and just nine interceptions. Thomas also rushed for 486 yards in leading the UO offense to a school record and national best 530.7 yards of total offense per game.

The 21-year-old from Houston, Tex., had a memorable debut for the Ducks in 2008. He entered the game in the second half and nearly led Oregon back from a 24-point fourth-quarter deficit against nationally ranked Boise State. He completed 13-of-25 passes for 210 yards and three touchdowns in the fourth quarter to set a school record for most passing yards and passing TDs by a freshman playing his first game.

The quarterback who wears No. 1 on his uniform may wind up No. 1 among all the great quarterbacks in Oregon history.

Pick A Letter

Pick one letter in each pair of letters to spell out the last name of an Oregon quarterback. For example, FT AI DF EY is FIFE. Answers on page 137.

1. RS EH AT MW   _____

2. FH AO RU NT SY   _____

3. AM IN LS HL ET RS   _____

4. OP MN AE CI LP   _____

5. BC RL EO MU ES HN ST   _____

6. MW AE PS OT DL EI   _____

7. DR IU EX OW NR   _____

8. BM AU ST GR RT AI TV EY   _____

9. FG EI ER CL ET DY   _____

10. BO GR BC EU AR KN   _____

Quarterbacks Word Search

Answers on page 138.

```
O  S  A  A  M  U  S  G  R  A  V  E  C  J  S
L  I  S  M  W  Z  Y  Z  R  E  N  R  U  T  T
S  I  M  T  A  D  O  D  B  A  R  N  E  S  U
O  Y  E  I  E  H  G  R  O  S  Z  T  U  O  O
N  R  W  N  L  L  N  E  W  Q  U  I  S  T  F
W  R  N  H  O  L  L  U  S  K  D  J  A  O  V
M  E  O  E  G  B  E  E  D  I  X  O  N  N  P
K  B  T  N  B  L  C  R  A  B  T  R  E  E  I
C  H  G  D  U  A  N  O  T  E  L  G  N  I  S
O  T  N  E  R  N  N  S  N  E  M  E  L  C  Z
S  I  I  R  N  C  E  E  G  A  D  N  U  R  B
T  M  R  S  T  H  L  J  H  M  A  S  O  L  I
A  S  R  O  Z  A  S  F  I  F  E  E  L  E  Y
S  V  A  N  B  R  O  C  K  L  I  N  W  J  H
W  A  H  S  I  D  N  S  A  M  O  H  T  H  H
```

BARNES	FEELEY	LUSK	OLSON
BERRY	FIFE	MAAS	POST
BLANCHARD	FOUTS	MASOLI	SHAW
BRUNDAGE	GRAZIANI	MILLER	SINGLETON
CLEMENS	GROSZ	MUSGRAVE	SMITH
COSTA	HARRINGTON	NELSON	STELLE
CRABTREE	HENDERSON	NEWQUIST	THOMAS
DIXON	JORGENSEN	O NEIL	TURNER
DUNHAM	KENNEDY	OGBURN	VAN BROCKLIN

Ogburn Sudoku

Use logic to fill in the boxes so every row, column and 2 x 3 box contains the letters O-G-B-U-R-N, in honor of Reggie Ogburn, the Ducks' double-threat quarterback in 1979-80. Solution on page 137.

			G	N	
N	U			B	
				R	N
O	R				
	N			U	O
		R	B		

Dave Grosz Sudoku

Use logic to fill in the boxes so every row, column and 3 x 3 box contains the letters D-A-V-E-G-R-O-S-Z, in honor of former Ducks quarterback Dave Grosz. Solution on page 139.

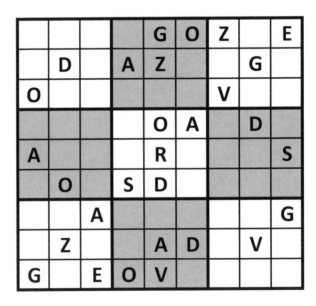

Crossing Patterns

Place the letters at the bottom of each grid into the empty squares to form the first and last names of six Oregon quarterbacks. Solutions on page 138.

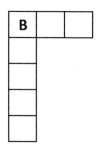

1. B E O R R Y

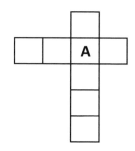

2. A J M N O S S

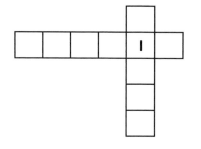

3. D D E N N O S X

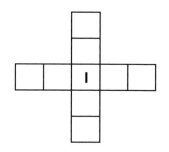

4. A H I K L M S T

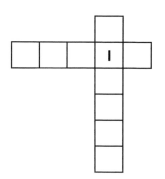

5. C E H L L M R R S

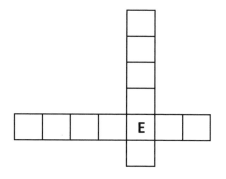

6. C E E K L L L M N N S

Quarterbacks Crossword
Solution on page 138.

Across

1. Ducks QB who appeared on the cover of *Sports Illustrated* on Sept. 29, 2003
5. UO starting QB between Ogbum and Jorgensen
9. Ducks QB who played 15 seasons with the Chargers and is in the Pro Football Hall of Fame
14. Computer image
15. Many a tournament
16. Concur with the head coach
17. Overly bookish sort
18. Fraternity party attire
19. Arm bones
20. Minnesota 2010 gubernatorial candidate
22. First-year player
24. Mariner (2 wds.)
26. First lady
27. Turkish title
30. Sunday night NFL game broadcaster from 1990-97
31. Atlas contents
34. Kind of cuisine
36. Conditional release from jail
38. First-rate player
39. All-American QB known as "The Dutchman" (2 wds.)
42. Football equipment
44. Single grain of corn
45. Reflect on a Ducks' loss
48. Cooking fat
49. Watch chain
52. "We're number ___!"
53. Returning player, briefly
55. Oregon's second largest city
57. Gobble up a Pegasus Pizza
60. PK Park foul line markers
61. "Bolero" composer
64. USC Trojans: Men of ___
66. Made a touchdown?
67. Other team
68. Latin 101 verb
69. Pedestal part
70. UO QB who played minor league baseball
71. Ducks QB who threw five TD passes vs. Stanford in 1997
72. UO football All-American QB in 1954 and baseball All-American OF (1954 & '55)

Down

1. Police officers: Eugene's ___
2. Eugene Generals, slangily
3. Arrange information
4. At the sound of the horn
5. Campus parking place
6. "Once ___ a time . . . "
7. Utah's state flower
8. Scoundrel
9. Locker room tap
10. Stare at the cheerleaders
11. Big coffee holder
12. Alternative drink at Starbucks
13. Observe
21. Former Rams QB, ___ Gabriel
23. ___ *Got a Secret*
25. Player's uniform
27. Auth. unknown
28. Tonic's partner at Turtles Bar & Grill
29. UO golfer's hole-in-one

32. Training table meat
33. Blackthorn fruits
35. Damaging precipitation
36. Rodeo cowboy, to a friend
37. Hosiery shade
39. Oregon barn topper
40. Player's joint with a cap
41. Slow down in the second half (2 wds.)
42. Mail place: Abbr.
43. Long, long time
46. 1984 Olympics gold medal sprinter, ___ Ashford
47. Gun, as an engine
49. Guy, slangily
50. Iroquois Indian
51. Grant
54. 50-Down pole
56. Prods the OSU fans
57. Audition tape
58. "Major" animal at the Children's Museum planetarium
59. Eugene's ___ Parks Plaza
61. ___ Lobster Restaurant
62. Start of a University of Idaho cheer: Gimme ___! (2 wds.)
63. Bother
65. Cry of success on a long FG

Quarterbacks Trivia

Answers on page 139.

1. Which quarterback had the most career rushing yards with 1,386?

2. Who played one summer in the Atlanta Braves organization before returning to Eugene to start at QB?

3. Who was the first UO quarterback to throw for 2,000+ yards in a season?

4. Which Ducks QB was the first in Pac-10 history to lead his team to three consecutive bowl victories?

5. Which Ducks QB scored the most points in his career?

6. Which former Oregon starting quarterback was the head coach of South Eugene High School from 2001-06?

7. Who holds the school records for passing yards and total offense in a career?

8. Which Ducks QB was the first player selected in the 1955 NFL Draft?

9. Who was the Pac-10 Offensive Player of the Year in 1998 after throwing for 3,763 yards and 32 touchdowns?

10. Who was the last UO QB to lead the team in rushing for a season?

11. Which Ducks QB appeared on the cover of *Sports Illustrated* after leading Oregon to an upset win over No. 3 Michigan in 2003?

12. Who was the UO quarterback in the Ducks' 1963 Sun Bowl win?

13. Which former Oregon quarterback won the NFL MVP award in 1960?

14. Where did Jeremiah Masoli play in the 2010 season?

15. Which Ducks quarterback had the most rushing yards in a season?

16. List these QBs in order by the year they started for Oregon, from most recent to earliest: Kellen Clemens, Joey Harrington, Mike Jorgensen, Jason Maas and Danny O'Neil.

17. Who is the only quarterback to lead the Ducks in passing yards four consecutive seasons?

18. Which Oregon QB is a sixth generation cattle rancher, whose family has 100 head of cattle in Burns, Ore.?

19. Who were the backup quarterbacks to Dan Fouts in 1972?

20. Who were the two QBs who shared the snaps in 1996 for a team that went 6-5, but did not go to a bowl game?

21. Which Ducks QB threw for the most yards in a game?

22. Joey Harrington threw six touchdown passes in a game twice. Who is the only other Ducks quarterback with six TD passes?

23. Who was the Oregon starting QB from 1975-77 when the Ducks won a total of nine games?

24. Who threw the longest pass in UO history, a 95-yarder caught by Bob Newland in 1970?

25. Who was Oregon's quarterback in the 1917 Rose Bowl win over Pennsylvania?

Darron Thomas

Short Yardage Crossword

Solution on page 140.

Across

1. Sheep's cry from the University farms
4. Manhandles the Huskies
6. Wiggles
8. Lubricate
9. Virile, like a UO football player
11. RB named UO's Most Outstanding Player in 2004 in a vote of the team
13. No longer on the plate at training table
14. Turn yellow, perhaps
15. Repeats
17. Parts of the field
18. College major

Down

1. PK Park base, slangily
2. Increaser
3. To whom a Muslim prays
4. Word in the Second Amendment
5. Breaks away?
6. Crusade for those who believe in 3-Down
7. Horse drawn carriages
8. Be in debt
10. "___ to Billie Joe"
12. Aquarium fish
16. Feedbag morsel

After solving the crossword puzzle, use the letters in the grid to answer the additional clue. Transfer the letters in numbered boxes to the corresponding blanks below. (Or answer the additional clue first to help you solve the crossword puzzle.)

Ducks RB who won the Texas HS 100-meter dash title in 2006

__ __ __ __ __
6 2 4 13 7

Chapter 4

Running Backs

LaMichael James has etched his name throughout the Oregon record book in just two seasons on the field. The third-place finisher in the 2010 Heisman Trophy voting as a sophomore, the 5-foot-9, 185-pounder could wind up with every rushing record in school history.

As a redshirt freshman in 2009, James ran for 1,546 yards, the most ever for a freshman in the Pac-10 Conference. He added a national best 1,731 yards in 2010. His career total of 3,277 rushing yards is just 19 yards shy of the school career record held by Derek Loville.

The Texarkana, Tex., native has scored 38 touchdowns (35 on the ground) and trails just Loville (45 career TDs) among non-kickers for points in a career. He also has caught 34 passes for 376 yards in two seasons.

James is the latest in a long line of great UO running backs. Other Oregon backs who earned all-America honors were Jake Leight (1945), Mel Renfro (1962-63), Bobby Moore (1971) and Jonathan Stewart (2007).

Statistically, others who have left a lasting impression on Ducks fans are Loville (1986-89), Terrance Whitehead (2002-05), Sean Burwell (1990-93), Ricky Whittle (1992-95), Jeremiah Johnson (2005-08), Maurice Morris (2000-01), Don Reynolds (1972-74), Onterrio Smith (2001-02), Reuben Droughns (1998-99), LeGarrette Blount (2008-09), Tony Cherry (1984-85) and Saladin McCullough (1996-97).

Earlier contributors were John Kitzmiller, 1928-30, who was elected to the College Football Hall of Fame; Mike Mikulak, 1931-33; "Tuffy" Leeman, 1932; Jay Graybeal, 1937-39; Earl Stelle, 1948-50; Jim Shanley, 1955-57; and Willie West, 1957-59.

Ifs and Thens

Complete this puzzle to reveal the name of an all-time great Ducks running back.

__	__	__	__	__		__	__	__	__	__	__	__
1	2	3	4	5		6	7	8	9	10	11	12

* If running back LaMichael James wore uniform number 21 in 2010, then the 4th letter is E; if he wore number 44, then the 10th letter is R.

* If Bobby Moore was the first Oregon player to rush for 1,000+ yards in a season, then the 1st letter is D; if it was Dick Winn, then the 3rd letter is S.

* If Tony Cherry was born in France, then the 6th letter is P; if it was Libya, then the 7th letter is O.

* If Jonathan Stewart was selected by the Carolina Panthers in the 1st Round of the 2008 NFL Draft, then the 11th letter is L; if it was the 4th Round, then the 5th letter is R.

* If Mel Renfro was part of a world record setting 440-yard relay team, then the 9th letter is I; if it was Pat Verutti, then the 12th letter is S.

* If LeGarrette Blount led the Ducks in rushing at the 2008 Holiday Bowl, then the 8th letter is R; if it was Jeremiah Johnson, then the 2nd letter is E.

* If Terrence Whiteland played with the Las Vegas Locomotives of the United Football League in 2009, then the 5th letter is K; if it was the Edmonton Eskimos of the Canadian Football League, then the 2nd letter is A.

* If Onterrio Smith transferred to Oregon from Michigan, then the 11th letter is T; if it was Tennessee, then the 10th letter is L.

* If Rueben Droughns won a championship ring at Super Bowl XLII with the New York Giants, then the 8th letter is V; if it was Ricky Whittle, then the 4th letter is O.

* If Saladin McCullough led the Pac-10 in rushing yards in 1997, then the 3rd letter is R; if he didn't, then the 7th letter is A.

* If Maurice Morris played two seasons at Oregon after transferring from a junior college, then the 12th letter is E; if he played four seasons at UO, then the 1st letter is H.

* If Don Reynolds had the longest run in school history (92 yards) in 1972, then the 9th letter is G; if it was Bob Smith in 1938, then the 6th letter is L.

Solution on page 140.

Running Backs Crossword

Solution on page 141.

Across

1. Auto
4. RBs Dick (1964-65) or Eric (1994-97)
8. Sports figure
12. Wait
13. Eugene Opera highlight
14. Steve Prefontaine distance, often
15. Recurring theme
16. Splinter group
17. Treated a sprained ankle
18. Like a fairy tale monster
20. Bagpiper's wear
22. Combined with Johnson for 2,203 rushing yards in 2008
23. Admiring the great plays
27. Merkley or Wyden: Abbr.
28. Comics shriek
30. Kenny Rowe or Terrell Turner
31. Chef Emeril's exclamation
32. Computer program with commercials
34. Swelling
36. "___ never work!"
39. Overtime Tavern, e.g.
40. Farm team
41. Borax Lake fish
43. Narcotic
46. Buffalo Exchange fluffy scarf
47. UO tennis player's shot
49. Drop the ball
50. "We ___ Family"
53. Aloha Bowl dress
55. First UO back to rush for 1,000+ yards in consecutive seasons
57. Table scraps

59. Eugene retirement community: Churchill ___
60. Not tricked by
63. Dalai ___
65. Team photographer's request
66. Close in on a team record
67. "Woe is me!"
68. Home run call: "___ it good-bye!"
69. Halftime lead, e.g.
70. UO's leading rusher in 1958 who played DB in the NFL and AFL for 9 years
71. "Are we there ___?"

Down

1. Citrus fruit
2. Chanterelle Restaurant farewell
3. Cultivated
4. Ore. neighbor
5. Intense anger at the ref
6. UO All-American DE, ___ Reed
7. "One ___ under God . . . "
8. Ducks' leading rusher in 2000-01
9. ___-tac-toe
10. Ruby Brew brew
11. UO punter, ___ Milburn
12. Cross between a Boxer and Beagle
15. Crowds following a championship game
19. Cafe Maroc lamb dish
21. Prospector's find
24. Wild goat
25. Back of the jersey identifier
26. FBI operative
29. 7th Avenue restaurant: Ali's ___

30. Like 13 Stories Down haunted house
32. Priest's robe
33. House of Records section
35. Anonymous John
36. Part of a nuclear arsenal, for short
37. Ten Commandments pronoun
38. Aloha Bowl feast
42. Cast aspersions on the Beavers
44. Quarterbacks' weapons
45. Russian revolutionist
48. Josey Wales, for one
50. Parlour Tattoo etcher
51. Cambodian currency
52. Latin 101 verb
54. The former Rashad
56. Chinese silk plant
58. Macy's after-Christmas event
59. Right on an Oregon map
60. Darron Thomas' uniform number
61. Actor ___ Beatty
62. Kind of team
64. "More" at Mission Mexican Restaurant

LaMichael James

What's in a Name?

An anagram is a word, phrase or sentence formed by rearranging all the letters of another word, phrase or sentence. For example, an anagram for the name of former UO running back RICKY WHITTLE is WRITE THICKLY. Rearrange the letters of these anagrams to come up with the first and last names of Oregon running backs. Solution on page 140.

1. MINOR THEORIST   _____

2. UNWELL BEARS   _____

3. WANDER RANCHES   _____

4. ONLY NODDERS   _____

5. OBEY OR BOMB   _____

6. CRY TO HENRY   _____

7. TROJANS WANT HATE   _____

8. ELM OR FERN   _____

9. JERK ON BANNER   _____

10. DARN BOWLINE   _____

He Said What?

Fill in the spaces with the words from the list to complete former NFL coach Jon Gruden's quote about Oregon's running attack. Solution on page 141.

"I DON'T _____ _____ THEIR _____

GUY COMES _____ . ONE _____ HE CAME

FROM _____ THE _____ AND _____

_____ AS THE PITCH _____ ."

ASTROTURF

FROM

GUY

KNOW

PITCH

SHOWED

TIME

UNDERNEATH

UP

WHERE

Who Am I? Sudoku

Use logic to fill in the boxes so every row, column and 2 x 3 box contains the letters of a memorable Oregon player. (Hint: He scored a school record 17 touchdowns in 2008.) When completed, the row indicated by the arrow will spell out the name correctly. Solution on page 140.

O					N
			B		
		O	U		T
T		N	O		
		B			
L					O

Dick James Sudoku

Use logic to fill in the grid below so that every row, column and 3 x 3 box contains the letters D-I-C-K-J-A-M-E-S, in honor of the Ducks' 1953 rushing leader. Solution on page 140.

I		D						A
	K		M				J	
				E				I
			K		E		I	
		M				C		
	E		D		S			
E				S				
	J				C		D	
C						E		M

Running Backs Trivia
Answers on page 141.

1. Who was the first Ducks running back to rush for 1,000+ yards in a season?

2. Since 1940, seven Ducks have led the conference in rushing. Name four of them.

3. Which two UO RBs were the first to run for 100+ yards in the same game? Hint: It was in 1960.

4. Ricky Whittle was part of two games with two running backs over 100 yards, one in 1992 and another in 1994. Who did he do it with?

5. Which UO running back was the MVP of the College All-Star Game in 1932 and was later inducted into the Pro Football Hall of Fame?

6. Who were the two Ducks to lead the team in rushing for four seasons?

7. Which UO RB has rushed for 100+ yards in a game the most times?

8. Who holds the school season record with 164.8 rushing yards per game?

9. Who set the school record with 285 rushing yards in one game?

10. Who holds the UO record for rushing yards in a bowl game with 253 in the 2007 Sun Bowl?

11. Which Oregon RB was the first to run for 200+ yards in a game?

12. Which four UO backs have run for 100+ yards in a game as a freshman, sophomore, junior and senior?

13. In the 1976-77 seasons, an Oregon player rushed for 100 yards in a game once. Who was he?

14. Who was the last player to run for 200+ yards in a game against the Ducks?

15. Which UO back set the school record with 45 carries in a 1999 game?

16. The Oregon record for rushing touchdowns in a game is held by Charles Taylor vs. Puget Sound in 1910. How many TDs did he score?

17. Of the players who played just two seasons at UO (not counting LaMichael James), which has the most career rushing yards?

18. Who rushed for the most TDs in their Oregon career?

19. LaMichael James set the UO freshman record with 1,546 rushing yards in 2009. Whose record did he break?

20. Who was the Oregon RB suspended for 10 games in 2009 for punching a Boise State player after a game?

21. Among the UO players with 2,000+ career yards, who has the highest average of 6.7 yards per carry?

22. Which Oregon back led the team in rushing three consecutive seasons, while doubling as a baseball star, finishing his career with school records for hits, runs batted in and stolen bases?

23. Who was the former UO back listed at 5-foot-7, and born in Libya, who played briefly with the Division champion San Francisco 49ers in 1986 and '87?

24. Which former Ducks running back earned a Super Bowl ring with the New York Giants and is now an assistant coach with Vukovi Beograd of Serbia in the Central European Football League?

25. Which running back signed a Letter of Intent with USC, but was released after a controversy surrounding his SAT scores, then scored five TDs for the Ducks vs. Arizona in 1996?

Running Backs Word Search

Answers on page 141.

```
S  M  I  T  H  Y  W  Y  T  R  A  W  E  T  S
K  O  G  V  F  J  E  L  T  T  I  H  W  M  Z
G  R  Y  E  F  I  O  L  E  E  G  C  M  E  R
C  R  D  R  O  U  G  H  N  S  R  I  P  C  O
G  I  A  U  K  U  R  B  N  A  D  O  S  H  B
K  S  E  T  I  R  A  U  E  S  H  L  O  A  L
V  R  H  T  V  E  Y  R  B  S  O  S  R  M  I
D  E  E  I  O  N  B  W  U  V  M  N  N  Y  N
H  D  T  Y  N  F  E  E  I  A  E  A  U  R  W
N  N  I  W  N  R  A  L  I  R  X  X  T  R  W
U  A  H  G  U  O  L  L  U  C  C  M  T  E  K
Y  S  W  R  B  E  L  L  W  A  Y  L  I  H  P
H  C  L  E  W  I  T  D  T  S  E  W  N  C  G
D  B  R  O  W  N  N  O  S  Y  A  R  G  Z  P
B  B  P  U  J  A  M  E  S  E  N  O  J  V  S
```

BARNER	JAMES	NOVIKOFF	SMITH
BELL	JOHNSON	NUTTING	STEWART
BENNETT	JONES	PHILYAW	VERUTTI
BROWN	LOVILLE	POWELL	WELCH
BURWELL	MCCULLOUGH	RENFRO	WEST
CHERRY	MCGEE	REYNOLDS	WHITEHEAD
DROUGHNS	MECHAM	ROBLIN	WHITTLE
GRAYBEAL	MOORE	SANDERS	WILLIAMS
GRAYSON	MORRIS	SHANLEY	WINN

Short Yardage Crossword

Solution on page 142.

Across

1. Ducks WR who was Joey Harrington's top target
6. Come into existence
10. Demetrius, Jaison and Cristin, e.g.
11. Amongst, poetically
12. Tree juice
13. "Ready, ___, go!"
15. NFLer
18. French hat
22. Part of the Ottoman Empire
24. State of destitution
25. WR who won UO's Most Improved Player Award in 2008

Down

1. Put on the coaching staff
2. S-shaped moldings
3. Tailgating trailer name
4. Genetic inits.
5. Thanksgiving veggies
6. Frequently, in verse
7. Game ticket info
8. Starbucks alternative drink
9. Sixth sense, for short
14. Basic belief
15. Last Greek consonant
16. Carry the ball
17. Cutlass or Delta 88
19. Deliver a tirade on the sideline
20. Mail Boxes ___
21. Kicker's prop
23. ___-tac-toe

After solving the crossword puzzle, use the letters in the grid to answer the additional clue. Transfer the letters in numbered boxes to the corresponding blanks below. (Or answer the additional clue first to help you solve the crossword puzzle.)

WR with more than 3,500 all-purpose yards for the Ducks from 1986-89

___ ___ ___ ___
6   18   9   20

Chapter 5

Receivers

With nine receptions in the BCS Championship Game, Oregon wide receiver Jeff Maehl brought his season total to 77, tying the school records for most catches in a season and career.

The senior from Paradise, Calif., didn't need those records to cement his status as one of the Ducks' all-time great receivers. But it certainly helps in debating the point.

Despite beginning at Oregon as a defensive back, Maehl wound up his college career with 178 catches for 2,311 yards and 24 touchdowns. His catches and TDs tied for the best in UO history; his yards were the seventh most.

Samie Parker is the Ducks star whose season and career records Maehl tied. Parker played for Oregon from 2000-03 and in the NFL from 2004-09.

The most well-known receiver in UO history is Bobby Moore (a.k.a. Ahmad Rashad). The Portland native began his Oregon career as a wide receiver (in 1969). He was moved to the backfield in 1970 and earned all-America honors as a RB in '71.

Rashad was the fourth pick in the 1972 NFL Draft, and played wide receiver in his 11-year pro career. He was a four-time Pro Bowl pick and finished his NFL career with 495 catches, 6,831 yards and 44 touchdowns.

Rashad parlayed his pro career into a long-time broadcasting career, working as a game analyst and studio host for football games, as well as working on a variety of other sports telecasts and non-sports shows.

Other top receivers in Ducks history include Lew Barnes (1983-85), Jayson Williams (2005-08), Keenan Howry (1999-2002), Demetrius Williams (2002-05), Cristin McLemore (1992-95), Bob Newland (1968-70) and Russ Francis (1973).

Paysinger Sudoku

Use logic to fill in the boxes so every row, column and 3 x 3 box contains the letters P-A-Y-S-I-N-G-E-R, in honor of former Ducks wide receiver Brian Paysinger. Solution on page 143.

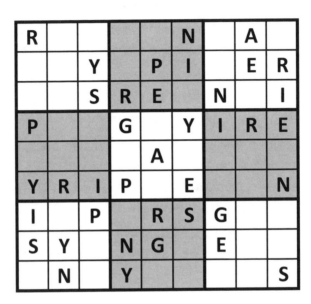

Offsides Sudoku

Now use the same letters (P-A-Y-S-I-N-G-E-R) and use logic to fill in the boxes so that every row and column contain those letters. The nine-letter "boxes" indicated by the solid lines aren't all square—they're offsides—but the solving rules remain the same. Solution on page 143.

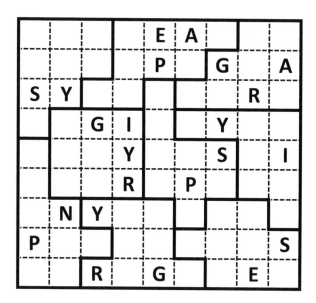

Receivers Crossword
Solution on page 144.

Across

1. Ducks All-Conference OL, ___ Snyder
5. UO's leading receiver in 2009-10
10. Receiver from 1986-89 who spent 8 years in the NFL
14. Locker room powder
15. Marche Cafe good-bye
16. Throw, as dice
17. Organic compound
18. Runs smoothly, as an engine
19. Study for final exams
20. "How about that!"
21. Skirt fold
22. Singles and doubles for the Ducks baseball team
23. UO track event
25. Poker ploy
27. Noted traitor, Benedict ___
30. Norway inlet
32. Carnivorous fish
33. Crater Lake fish
34. Maid's cloth
37. French father
38. Taste of India lentil dishes
39. Baylor's home
40. Put into words
41. Tim Lincecum, e.g.
42. Bishop's hat
43. Jellied garnish
44. Sixth Street Grill salad bar item
45. Add up
47. Wolf's sound
48. Sprightly
49. Basket material
52. Charged particle
55. Term paper list abbr.

56. Asian starlings
57. Be next to
59. Marine eagle
60. Ducks RB, ___ Crenshaw
61. Dermatologist's concern
62. Ducks' top receiver in 1977, Ken ___
63. Had 8 catches for 125 yards in 2008 Holiday Bowl
64. Peddle UO T-shirts

Down

1. Had some salmon at Sakura
2. "Drat!"
3. Training room balm ingredient
4. WR with 10 catches in the 1995 Rose Bowl
5. Did Rand McNally's job
6. Game ticket category, often
7. Emerald Isle
8. Zeus' wife
9. Glistening
10. Briggs Hill's special flower
11. Former tennis pro, ___ Becker
12. Make the fans jubilant
13. UO shade trees
24. SW Oregon river
26. College major
27. Nile snakes
28. Ducks' 1942 Outstanding Player Award winner, Floyd ___
29. ___ a soul
30. Swiss currency
31. Shock
33. Ring of Fire Restaurant cuisine
34. Pacific Continental Bank posting
35. Taiwan-based computer maker
36. Bloody

38. UO sheepskins
39. WR Demetrius or Jaison
41. Cookie selling org.
42. Kitten's cry
43. Former British PM
44. Victoria's Secret buy
45. Aquarium fish
46. Oregon Zoo big ape
47. Valentine symbol
48. Chick's sound

50. In ___ (playing together)
51. Prefix with China
53. Eugene Symphony woodwind
54. Partner of void
58. Business card abbr.

Dynamic Duos

The names of two pass catchers who were teammates have been combined on each line. The letters of each name are in the correct order, but you need to break apart the names to come up with the Dynamic Duos. Answers on page 143.

2009 MADICEHLKSON _____ _____

2005 WIFILLINLAMEYS _____ _____

2001 HOWILWRLISY _____ _____

1997 JOSPHNENSOCEN _____ _____

1993 TDEADAWILTEER _____ _____

1989 HARREIGATZUING _____ _____

1985 DEBBARISSNESCHOP _____ _____

1981 MOHOGENSERSEN _____ _____

1977 VINPACENTGE _____ _____

1973 PAFRANLMCIS _____ _____

Barnes Sudoku

Use logic to fill in the boxes so every row, column and 2 x 3 box contains the letters B-A-R-N-E-S, in honor of Lew Barnes, the Ducks' standout receiver from 1983-85. Solution on page 142.

		N	R	E	
	E	B	A		
		S			
			S		
		R	N	A	
	N	A	E		

Receivers Word Search

Answers on page 144.

```
J  Y  X  H  U  P  A  R  T  T  O  C  S  T  M
P  A  L  M  C  L  E  M  O  R  E  S  I  H  O
L  G  R  I  F  F  I  N  G  E  A  U  M  C  S
C  R  E  S  S  S  M  A  I  L  L  I  W  E  E
R  B  U  N  K  E  R  P  G  I  R  A  A  P  R
B  J  A  C  K  S  O  N  K  W  R  K  L  S  W
P  O  H  C  S  S  I  B  E  D  C  L  L  E  K
A  N  T  I  G  T  M  D  N  A  L  W  E  N  H
R  E  E  S  J  C  T  C  Y  E  H  O  W  R  Y
K  S  R  O  C  H  L  E  W  D  L  H  E  A  M
E  E  B  A  O  H  L  R  K  R  E  U  A  B  P
R  E  L  M  J  T  U  S  I  C  N  A  R  F  A
E  L  A  I  R  B  C  L  R  E  I  T  Z  U  G
E  S  T  A  W  I  L  L  E  N  E  R  M  Q  E
J  O  H  N  S  O  N  Z  J  R  E  V  O  T  S
```

BARNES	GLASS	MCCALL	RICKETTS
BAUER	GRIFFIN	MCLEMORE	SCHULER
BRETHAUER	HARTLEY	MOSER	SCOTT
BUNKER	HOWRY	NEWLAND	SPECHT
BURWELL	IMWALLE	OBEE	STOVER
CRESS	JACKSON	PAGE	THOMAS
DEADWILER	JOHNSON	PALM	WARD
DEBISSCHOP	JONES	PARKER	WILLENER
FRANCIS	MAEHL	REITZUG	WILLIAMS

63

Receivers Trivia
Answers on page 144.

1. Which tight end lettered just one season at Oregon, but was a first round draft pick of the New England Patriots in 1975?

2. Which wide receiver completed his college career in 1970 as UO's all-time receptions leader?

3. Who is the last Ducks player to lead the conference in pass receiving?

4. Which former UO receiver played in an exhibition basketball game with the Philadelphia '76ers?

5. Who holds the Oregon record with 16 catches in a game? Hint: It was in 2003.

6. Who holds the Oregon record with 242 receiving yards in a game? Hint: It was in 1998.

7. Who was the first Ducks player with 2,000+ career receiving yards?

8. Which UO receiver is the only one with four touchdown catches in a game?

9. Rank these players, most to least, by how many catches they had in their UO career: Ed Dickson, Bobby Moore, Terry Obee, Demetrius Williams, Jaison Williams.

10. Which two receivers share the Oregon record with 77 catches in a season?

11. Who holds the Oregon record with 1,123 receiving yards in a season?

12. Who is the last player to lead the Ducks in receptions three consecutive seasons?

13. When was the last time two Ducks had 100+ receiving yards in the same game?

14. From 2003 through 2007, the Ducks had a wide receiver selected in the NFL Draft each year. Name them.

15. Which UO tight end was an All-American in 1931, then was named to the NFL's 1930s All-Decade Team?

16. Who am I?
    * I was an All-American tight end for Oregon in 1934.
    * I played for the Detroit Lions in the NFL for five years.
    * I coached the Air Corps' Randolph Field Flyers to a 7-7 tie vs. Texas in the 1944 Cotton Bowl.
    * I was inducted into the UO Athletics Hall of Fame in 1997.
    * I was chosen by *The Register-Guard* to UO's All-Time team.

17. Who was the Ducks' All-American receiver in 1985 who played for the Bears, Falcons and Chiefs in the NFL, but had just four career receptions as a pro?

18. Which UO receiver played for the Baltimore Ravens from 2006-09 and the Cleveland Browns in 2010?

19. Who was the Ducks TE named to the Academic All-Conference first team in 2008?

20. Jeff Maehl received first-team All-Pac-10 honors in 2010. Prior to him, who was the last Oregon wide receiver to earn All-Pac-10 first team honors?

21. That same season, the Ducks had the first team All-Pac-10 tight end. Who was he?

22. Which receiver was known as "K-How?"

23. Which Ducks WR ran a 10.18 100-meter dash time for UO's track team and qualified for the 2004 U.S. Olympic Trials?

24. Which player, who was on the Ducks' broadcast team from 2001-06, set the Oregon school record (since broken) for most receptions in a season by a tight end with 40 catches in 1986?

25. Which wide receiver, who led the team in catches in 1994 and '95, caught 10 passes in the 1995 Rose Bowl?

Building Blocks

Read the clues and fill in the appropriate boxes. The answer to
the second clue is the answer to the first clue, plus one letter.
The answer to the third clue is the answer to the second clue,
plus one letter. And so on. (The order of the letters may change.)
Solution on page 143.

1. Letter on a Duck's helmet
2. Place where Ducks get their
    injured knees repaired, for
    short
3. State abbr.
4. Leading vote getter in
    Oregon in 2000 U.S.
    Presidential race
5. Monsters in a fairy tale at
    Smith Family Bookstore
6. UO tight end who also
    played FB and DE from
    2000-02

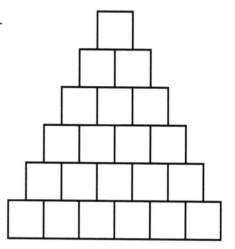

Change Ups

Change one letter in each word to spell the first and last names
of Oregon receivers who led the team in receiving for a season.
Solution on page 143.

1. MERRY OBOE
2. NEW BARGES
3. GREW LOSER
4. RINKY CARD
5. DEN CAGE
6. BIB BALM

Short Yardage Crossword

Solution on page 146.

Across

1. Shoulder or hip protector
4. Top O-lineman for the Ducks in 1999, Deke ___
8. Roster column heading
9. Mrs. Bush 43
10. Fond du ___, Wis.
11. Admittance to the game
12. Namely (2 wds.)
14. UO pitching stat
15. 18-wheeler
18. Long (for)
20. Inhale the popcorn aroma
23. Watch the Ducks score 60 points: Ooh and ___
25. Perpendicular to the keel
26. Halves in a game
27. Top O-lineman for the Ducks in 1997, Seaton ___
28. Orange Bowl clock setting

Down

1. Buddy
2. Tiny type size in the sports section
3. Home designer's concern
4. Team catchphrase
5. One of six in an inning
6. Mess up pass coverage
7. Dissenting vote in the Oregon Senate
9. Aloha Bowl floral necklace
13. Lie in wait
16. All worked up over the officiating
17. Chews like a Beaver
19. UO campus shade tree
20. Bummed about a Ducks loss
21. Lundquist College of Business graduate deg.
22. Sushi Ya fish
24. On a roll, like the UO offense

After solving the crossword puzzle, use the letters in the grid to answer the additional clue. Transfer the letters in numbered boxes to the corresponding blanks below. (Or answer the additional clue first to help you solve the crossword puzzle.)

OG/OT who was the Ducks' top offensive lineman in 2000 and '01

___ ___ ___ ___ ___
 2   27 23   4   20

Chapter 6

Offensive Linemen

Through the years, Oregon has had three offensive linemen earn consensus all-America honors: Steve Barnett (1961-62), Tom Drougas (1971) and Gary Zimmerman (1983).

Barnett is one of just two Ducks to earn all-American status on the field and in the classroom. The tackle was the key blocker for running back Mel Renfro and quarterback Bob Berry. He played two seasons in the NFL.

Drougas opened holes for running back Bobby Moore and protected quarterback Dan Fouts. The tackle from Beaverton, Ore., was a first-round pick in the 1972 NFL Draft and played five years of professional football.

Zimmerman was named the Pac-10 Conference's Offensive Lineman of the Year and received the rare honor of being named the conference's Player of the Week following a 1983 Oregon victory over California. The tackle from Fullerton, Calif., went on to star in the NFL for 12 seasons and was a seven-time Pro Bowl pick. He was elected to the Pro Football Hall of Fame in 2008.

Other Oregon offensive linemen of note are Jordan Holmes (2007-10), Max Unger (2004-08), Enoka Lucas (2003-06), Adam Snyder (2000-04), John McKean (1969-71), Mark Richards (1963-65), Dave Tobey (1963-65), Mickey Ording (1960-62), Ron Snidow (1960-62), Dave Urell (1958-60), Bob Peterson (1957-59), Bob Grottkau (1956-58), Harry Mondale (1955-57), Jack Patera (1951-54), Ron Pheister (1952-54), Chester Daniels (1948), Brad Ecklund (1946-48), Jim Stuart (1938-40), Del Bjork (1934-36), Austin Colbert (1928-30), George Stadelman (1927-29), Gene Shields (1923-25), Carl Vonder Ahe (1921-23), Bill Steers (1917-20), Earl Leslie (1919-21), Ken Bartlett (1914-16), Jake Risley (1914-17), W.C. Snyder (1914-16) and John Beckett (1913-16).

O-Line Word Search

Solution on page 147.

```
S  V  H  N  A  G  R  O  M  H  K  S  A  H  V
L  Q  M  G  W  U  T  I  L  U  N  G  H  N  F
N  H  A  K  U  N  Z  M  A  N  X  Y  K  N  O
T  I  U  B  G  A  C  A  S  T  L  E  I  L  P
C  D  R  G  A  M  B  D  E  A  N  D  X  G  A
H  Y  E  F  H  R  L  M  D  D  R  B  Y  I  E
Y  R  R  J  W  E  T  W  A  A  N  C  F  L  H
G  E  L  Y  I  M  S  L  H  T  O  P  H  B  R
E  D  L  H  G  M  L  E  E  L  S  I  L  E  B
K  G  S  S  G  I  T  S  U  T  T  O  R  R  R
N  R  T  X  I  Z  V  E  C  G  T  R  N  T  E
I  E  O  O  N  R  E  H  T  Y  A  M  Q  O  N
Z  B  K  J  S  E  K  Y  D  C  M  E  O  B  I
C  E  E  O  B  E  L  S  T  U  A  R  T  E  T
T  W  S  U  O  P  U  T  G  M  O  A  L  Y  S
```

ARCHER	GILBERT	MATTSON	STOKES
BARTLETT	GREGG	MAURER	STUART
BELISLE	HARDIN	MAYTHER	TEAGUE
BJORK	HUGHES	MORGAN	TOBEY
CARTER	HUNT	RHEA	TUPOU
CASTLE	KENDALL	RISLEY	WEBER
DALY	KUNZMAN	SHIELDS	WIGGINS
DEAN	LUNG	STAMBAUGH	ZIMMERMAN
DYKES	MATSON	STINER	ZINKE

Snyder Sudoku

Use logic to fill in the boxes so every row, column and 2 x 3 box contains the letters S-N-Y-D-E-R, in honor of former Ducks offensive lineman Adam Snyder. Solution on page 146.

Y			D		
		S	N		R
S		N	R		
		Y	S		E
N		E	Y		
		D			N

Floyd Rhea Sudoku

Use logic to fill in the grid below so that every row, column and 3 x 3 box contains the letters F-L-O-Y-D-R-H-E-A, in honor of guard Floyd Rhea, chosen UO's Most Outstanding Player in 1944. Solution on page 147.

H				A				D
			R		O			
		F		E		Y		
	R						A	
A		D				H		F
	L						E	
		R		H		E		
			D		F			
O				L				R

O-Line Name Grid

These offensive linemen's names are listed in alphabetical order according to length. Fit them into their proper places in the Grid. We've started your solving by placing the name WEBER (make certain you scratch it off the list). Now look for a 5-letter name that has a W as the third letter. Continue working that way until you've filled in the Grid. But be careful. There might be a name that seems to work in more than one place, but each name is used just once. Solution is on page 148.

5 Letters	6 Letters	7 Letters
BJORK	CASTLE	DANIELS
BOWIE	KNEBEL	MAYTHER
DOTUR	MATSON	MONDALE
HUSKO	MAURER	
LUCAS	MCKEAN	**8 Letters**
THRAN	PATERA	PETERSON
TOBEY	SNYDER	PHEISTER
URELL	STOKES	RICHARDS
WEBER	STUART	
ZINKE	WEAVER	**9 Letters**
		DAUGHERTY
		STADELMAN
		VONDERAHE

Offensive Linemen Crossword

Solution on page 148.

Across

1. Middle of March
5. Eugene eatery name, with D.
8. Ducks T who played with the Bengals from 1976-78
12. Oregon Marching Band instrument
13. "___ we there yet?"
14. Willow twig
16. First African-American player in MLB's Amer. League, Larry ___
17. Burger Lovers sandwich, for short
18. Son of your brother
20. Hog's home
22. Tie the knot
23. Wish undone
24. Ducks OG with the Philadelphia Eagles, Fenuki ___
27. Dorm cafeteria carrier
29. Flower holder
30. Darron Thomas' uniform number
31. Copy company
33. Eugene's county
34. "___ to Billie Joe"
35. Clearasil target
36. Plum's center
37. Chop off
38. All-American OT who was the 1st pick of the Colts in 1972
40. Neighbor of a Vietnamese
43. Ducks pitcher's stat
44. One of the Bobbsey twins
45. Antiquated
46. June 6, 1944
48. Milk dispenser
50. *The Matrix* hero
51. Stick-to-itiveness, like a Ducks player

52. Training room hot tubs
53. Winner of the Ed Moshofsky Award from 2006-08 as the Ducks' top O-lineman
55. Thumbs-up
56. Zimmerman has three
57. Utah Stars' org.
58. Canal site
60. Airline's home base
62. Bit of sweat on a player
66. Team doc
67. Eugene's st.
68. Wild party
69. UO Freshman All-American OG in 2009, Carson ___
70. Dickson or Reed, e.g.
71. Scottish hillside

Down

1. Babyface lyric: "You said ___ be alright . . . "
2. Pair, like Thomas and Maehl
3. Flow's partner
4. Final approval, as the head coach (2 wds.)
5. Newborn
6. WWW address
7. Get in an NCAA basketball pool
8. Sweetie pie
9. Brought into play
10. Barely beat
11. Persian Gulf capital
15. Recycle a previous year's play
19. Pee-___ League
21. Heisman Trophy Award Dinner formal wear
22. Fast Track Car Wash option
24. Hammer or saw
25. Word processing command

26. Peek
27. Donald Duck's nephews, e.g.
28. Oregon State Capitol feature
29. King Estate Winery tank
32. Poet ___ Pound
33. Fleur-de-___
36. Dorm window section
38. Dishwasher cycle
39. Gallivants
40. Special teams OL: ___ snapper
41. Sheltered from the wind
42. Emanation coming from an old locker
43. Dig in at training table
46. Fantasize about a national championship

47. Duck rights holder
48. Downs' opposite
49. Massage a player's back
51. Swindle
52. Tackle impact sound
54. Wealthy one
56. Mideast ruler
57. Sacked out
59. Goings-on at Autzen Stadium
60. Garden tool
61. Big coffee holder
63. Drop the ball
64. Turkish title
65. Turn green or yellow, perhaps

Offensive Line Trivia
Answers on page 145.

1. Who was the two-time All-American who anchored the offensive line for the 1960 squad that set a school record (since broken) with 3,671 total yards?

2. Which Oregon All-American lineman was chosen in the first round of the 1972 NFL Draft after blocking for Bobby Moore?

3. Who started a school-record 51 consecutive games from 2004-08?

4. Who was named the Pac-10's top offensive lineman in 1983?

5. Who was the NFL's Offensive Lineman of the Year in 1997 with the Denver Broncos?

6. The Ducks' annual award for the top offensive lineman is named the Ed Moshofsky Award. Who is Ed?

7. Since the Moshofsky Award began in 1992, who is the only three-time winner?

8. Who was the last O-lineman named the Ducks' Most Outstanding Player? Hint: It was in 1965.

9. Who was the Oregon guard in 1992-93 whose daughter is on the basketball team at the University of Arizona?

10. Who was the Ducks' 6-foot-7, 334-pound guard from 1990-94 who played one game for the Indianapolis Colts in the NFL, then five seasons with the B.C. Lions in the CFL?

11. The Ducks had an offensive tackle selected by the Pittsburgh Steelers in the 1997 NFL Draft, then didn't have another offensive lineman chosen until 2005 by the San Francisco 49ers. Who were the Ducks' O-linemen selected in those two drafts?

12. Who am I?
    * I was a center for the Ducks and earned all-conference honors three times.
    * I was a Marine Corps Golden Gloves boxing champion.
    * I was a two-time All-Pro NFL player.
    * I was an assistant coach under Tom Landry for the first Dallas Cowboys team.
    * I appeared in the football movie *North Dallas Forty*.

13. Which Ducks center (1993-97), who graduated from Gonzaga Law School, is now an attorney in Seattle?

14. Who was Oregon's guard from 1996-98 who became a tight ends coach at Boise State?

15. Name four of the five offensive linemen voted by *The Oregonian* readers to UO's All-Decade Team (2000-09).

16. Who was the offensive line coach on the 2010 squad?

17. Who was the walk-on center who worked at a titanium casting plant after high school to gain weight before enrolling at UO? He wound up earning the team's Offensive Lineman of the Year Award twice.

18. Which former Ducks OT is now a two-way star for the Umpqua Valley Knights of the Oregon Football League? He was chosen as the 2010 league MVP.

19. In which city did center Enoka Lucas (2002-05) attend high school?

20. Who was the Ducks' O-lineman who started at LT, LG and RT, and earned first team All-Pac-10 honors in 2009?

21. The Wil Gonyea Award is given annually to the Ducks' Most Inspirational Player. Which offensive lineman won that award in 2001, in addition to being named an Academic All-American twice?

22. Which Oregon offensive tackle self-reported receiving improper benefits from a potential agent and served a one-game suspension in 2008?

23. Which Ducks' OT was selected in the seventh round of the 2008 NFL Draft by the Carolina Panthers and is listed among the *Who's Who of Great American Jewish Athletes*?

24. Who was the Ducks' OT drafted by the Philadelphia Eagles in 1990 who played at Palomar Community College before enrolling at UO?

25. Who is the only UO player to appear in the College All-Star Game twice?

Six Down Linemen

Brian Castle was an offensive lineman who played at Oregon from 1980-82. Use logic to complete the 6 x 6 grid so that each row and each column contain the letters C-A-S-T-L-E. Solution on page 146.

	C	L			
S			C		A
	A				E
		T			C
A		C	S		L
	S			E	

Double Switch

The first and last names of 10 UO offensive linemen have been split into two-letter segments. The letters in each segment are in order, but the segments have been mixed up. Put together the pieces in each line to come up with the players' names. Answers on page 147.

1. CK ST TZ EI NI   _____

2. MA NG XU ER   _____

3. MD RO TO AS UG   _____

4. TT NE AR EB EV ST   _____

5. SC ID HM AN RY   _____

6. YO ON RK CA RS   _____

7. EN OK UC AL AS   _____

8. DA WI OX VE LC   _____

9. MA JI DA MS   _____

10. KE ED EN MO   _____

Ducks Fill-in

Fill in the missing letter for each of the words listed. Be careful, because all of the words can be completed with more than one letter. Transfer the correct letter to the corresponding line so that the result is the name of the Ducks offensive lineman who in 2010 won the Bob Officer Award, presented to a player who has made a major contribution toward the success of the football program despite physical adversity. Solution on page 147.

__ . __ .   __   __   __   __   __   __
 1   2   3   4   5   6   7   8

1. __ ATCH

2. B __ AT

3. FA __ E

4. TE __ M

5. L __ NE

6. LO __ E

7. SCOR __

8. __ USH

Short Yardage Crossword

Solution on page 149.

Across

1. Oregon State Legislature voting group
5. UO LB from 1973-76 who is the football coach at Churchill High School
9. Overhaul the defense
10. Black-and-white cookie at Albertson's
11. Mideast port
12. Poetic foot
13. Ducks backup QB, Nate ___
15. Ducks DB who returned an interception for a TD vs. Washington in 1994
17. Short Japanese poem
18. Pugilist's weapon
19. Rip apart a defense
23. Poker pot starter
24. 14-14, e.g.
25. DE who earned All-America honors on the field and in the classroom
26. ___ record (2 wds.)

Down

1. Victoria's Secret purchase
2. Was ahead in the game
3. "___ to Billie Joe"
4. Egotistical
5. Sweat beads
6. Muse of poetry
7. Macho dude, like a defensive tackle
8. High shot in tennis
14. Symbol of sturdiness
15. Complain about a ref's call
16. Waste maker
18. Wide's partner
20. Night before the big game
21. Volleyball court divider
22. Modern courtroom evidence

After solving the crossword puzzle, use the letters in the grid to answer the additional clue. Transfer the letters in numbered boxes to the corresponding blanks below. (Or answer the additional clue first to help you solve the crossword puzzle.)

The Ducks' leading tackler from 1990-92

___ ___ ___ ___ ___ ___ ___
18 11 19 15 24 2   8

Chapter 7

Defensive Players

It may have been Oregon's flashy and fast offense that garnered most of the attention in 2010. Rightly so. But the oft-overlooked defense was no slouch. Oregon led the Pac-10 in rushing defense, pass efficiency defense and opponent third-down conversions. The defense recorded two shutouts and came up big when it had to: Oregon yielded just 27 points in the 13 fourth quarters combined.

The stars of Oregon's 2010 defensive squad were linebacker Casey Matthews, defensive lineman Brandon Bair and defensive backs Talmadge Jackson and Cliff Harris. They were the latest in a long line of defensive standouts for Oregon.

UO defenders who were named all-Americans were: DE Nick Reed (2008), DT Haloti Ngata (2005), CB Alex Molden (1995), SS Chad Cota (1994), CB Herman O'Berry (1994), CB Chris Oldham (1989) and DB Jim Smith (1967).

The best former Oregon defensive player in the NFL may have been Dave Wilcox. A guard on offense and end on defense, Wilcox played at UO in 1962-63. He switched to linebacker in the pros and starred for the San Francisco 49ers for 11 seasons. He was a seven-time Pro Bowl pick and was inducted into the Pro Football Hall of Fame. What was the secret to his success? "What I do best is not let people block me," Wilcox said. "I just hate to be blocked."

Other top defenders included DT Vince Goldsmith (the 1980 Pac-10 Lineman of the Year), LB Tom Graham (the school record holder in tackles with 433 from 1969-71), DE Saul Patu (who holds the UO career record with 53 tackles for loss from 1997-2000) and DB George Shaw (who had 18 career interceptions and also starred at QB from 1951-54).

Byrd is the Word

Jarius Byrd was an All-Pac 10 defensive back in 2008. He was the co-Freshman of the Year in the conference in 2006, the Defensive MVP of the '08 Holiday Bowl and the 2nd Round pick of the Buffalo Bills in the 2009 NFL Draft. The letters B-Y-R-D can be arranged to form 24 different combinations. Here are 21 of those combinations. Which three combinations are missing? Answer on page 148.

BYDR	BYRD	DBYR	RYDB	RBDY	BDRY	BRDY
DRYB	RDBY	RYBD	YBDR	BDYR	DRBY	YDBR
YRDB	YRBD	YBRD	YDRB	DBRY	DRYB	RDYB

Who Am I? Sudoku

Use logic to fill in the boxes so every row, column and 3 x 3 box contains the letters of a memorable Oregon player. (Hint: Despite standing just 5-foot-11, this defensive tackle was a two-time All-Pac 10 player.) When completed, the row indicated by the arrow will spell out the name correctly. Solution on page 149.

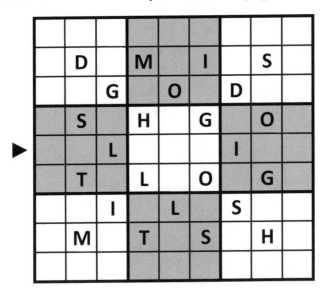

Defensive Players Word Search
Answer on page 150.

```
M  T  A  L  B  O  T  R  E  K  C  I  R  E  Z
A  E  I  X  E  Q  V  F  A  R  W  E  L  L  S
T  N  L  U  U  G  N  U  H  C  M  V  H  G  I
S  T  S  H  E  R  M  A  N  Z  O  A  T  T  R
O  S  E  T  E  E  G  I  P  S  O  N  I  P  M
N  N  V  Y  Y  M  I  M  T  R  R  D  M  S  O
V  R  O  E  O  R  H  N  E  C  E  I  S  B  N
M  A  R  S  E  B  S  U  N  Y  H  V  P  E  P
S  E  G  H  K  I  W  H  D  E  E  E  I  E  H
L  K  S  R  J  C  A  R  A  E  R  R  L  K  S
E  A  O  N  O  T  A  E  H  W  T  M  L  L  K
K  K  C  I  O  L  D  J  A  C  F  Z  I  E  C
I  A  N  C  L  L  T  R  E  B  L  U  H  Y  U
M  A  H  A  R  G  D  E  Y  P  I  E  P  E  R
Y  H  M  O  R  E  T  T  I  B  A  G  B  I  T
```

ASHER	GRAHAM	MEYER	SHAW
BEEKLEY	HUDETZ	MIKELS	SHERMAN
BOYETT	HULBERT	MITCHELL	SIRMON
BYRD	JACKSON	MOORE	SMITH
CHUNG	KAUMEYER	MORETTI	TALBOT
COSGROVE	KEARNS	PHILLIPS	TRUCKS
COTA	MALLARD	PIEPER	VANDIVER
FARWELL	MATSON	RENNIE	WARD
GIPSON	MEHL	RICKERT	WHEATON

Defenders Crossword

Solution on page 151.

Across

1. CB who won the Defensive MVP Award at the 2008 Holiday Bowl
5. UO All-American safety who played for the Panthers, Saints, Colts and Rams in the NFL
9. Former UO CB who had 26 NFL interceptions from 1976-84
14. Man of immoral conduct
15. Mimicked
16. Vietnam's capital
17. Eugene-born singer-songwriter, ___ Gilbert
18. Ahead on the scoreboard
19. Threw in
20. West Coast contemporary furniture name
22. Portland-based conservative talk show host, ___ Larson
24. Part of a football uniform
27. Fender blemish
28. UO fraternity letter
31. Olympics chant
32. Put up a fight
35. Rushes?
36. Lord's Prayer pronoun
37. UO grad.
38. Sleep activity
39. Puzzle theme
42. *A Christmas ___*
45. Small whirlpool
46. Beast of burden
49. Similar (to)
50. Team chaplain
52. White House nickname
53. AAA Oregon handout
54. Myrmo & ___, Inc.
55. Radio84 blast from the past
57. Obligation
58. "What've you been ___?" (2 wds.)

60. Run through (2 wds.)
63. Water carrier
65. Corduroy feature
69. Harder to find
70. Roaring Rapids Pizza Co. fixture
71. 21-21
72. Ducks DT selected by Baltimore in 1st round of the 2006 Draft
73. Former UO safety whose cousin is Maurice Jones-Drew
74. DE who finished career with a school-record 29.5 sacks

Down

1. Female runner's equipment: sports ___
2. "Silent Night" adjective
3. Ducks baseball score
4. Passed out cards
5. Storm preceder
6. Not covered by the defense
7. Oolong, for one
8. Confuses
9. Backup QB's sideline work
10. Young fellows
11. 1st-___-10
12. Fish eggs
13. Youngster
21. Tel Aviv's country
23. Picnic pest
24. UO track & field event: shot ___
25. Ducks baseball bat wood
26. Oregon Senate dissenting vote
27. Poor light quality
28. Eugene store: Sweet Potato ___
29. Last word of "America, the Beautiful"
30. Doctrine: Suffix
33. Santa's little helper
34. Take to court
35. Mins. and mins.

38. Plant disease
39. UO football and baseball star of 1975, ___ Reynolds
40. Banned pesticide
41. Tokyo, formerly
42. Former Miami Dolphins head coach, ___ Cameron
43. Letters before an alias
44. Oak Hill Cemetery tombstone letters
46. Autzen Stadium sign: First ___
47. Hit the slopes at Timberline Lodge
48. "Told ya!"
50. Poker prize
51. Be that as it may
54. Kendall Toyota model
56. Decrease
57. "Portland, Oregon" singers Loretta Lynn and Jack White, e.g.
58. Computer operator
59. Remain unsettled
60. Big coffee holder
61. Slump off a receiver
62. Ducks pitcher's stat
64. Egg cells
66. Eugene's 13th or 18th, among others
67. Donut shop name on Barger Drive
68. Tukuafu or Wrighster, e.g.

Build the Name

Use the letter groups—one at the beginning and one at the end—to build the names of former UO defensive stars. Each letter group will be used once. Answers on page 149.

AN BA BRA CO EE ER ETH EY FLE GOL
HI IPS ITH MO ON PH PHI SON TI WH

1. _____ NIS _____

2. _____ TCH _____

3. _____ EAT _____

4. _____ NTL _____

5. _____ DSM _____

6. _____ LEM _____

7. _____ LDR _____

8. _____ ILL _____

9. _____ RET _____

10. _____ NDI _____

Mikels Sudoku

Use logic to fill in the boxes so every row, column and 2 x 3 box contains the letters M-I-K-E-L-S, in honor of the Ducks' standout linebacker, Jerry Mikels, who led the team in tackles in 1983 and '85. Solution on page 149.

		K			
	L	E	M		
		L	I	S	
	S	M	E		
		I	L	E	
			K		

Defenders Trivia

Answers on page 149.

1. Which defensive back started the first game of his true freshman season at UO in 1972 and wound up with 13 interceptions in his collegiate career? Hint: He won a Super Bowl ring while a member of the San Francisco 49ers.

2. Who was the Ducks' All-American defensive tackle who as a high school athlete was the No. 1 ranked shot putter in the nation?

3. Who was the College Football Hall of Fame defensive back from Oregon known as "The Flying Dutchman?"

4. Which Ducks' DB was an All-American in 1995 and played nine seasons in the NFL with the Saints, Chargers and Lions?

5. Who was the Ducks DT from Tonga who won the Morris Trophy as the Pac-10's top defensive lineman in 2005?

6. Which Oregon defender led the nation with five fumble recoveries in 2008?

7. Which former Oregon back played in 10 consecutive Pro Bowls and in four Super Bowls?

8. Which UO star led the nation in interceptions in 1951, but is better known as the team's quarterback?

9. Which Oregon DB known as "Yazoo" was the team's MVP in 1967?

10. Who was the UO redshirt freshman who returned an interception 97 yards for a touchdown against Washington in 1994 to put the Ducks into the Rose Bowl?

11. Which former Oregon player and Pro Football Hall of Fame member was the first defensive lineman to earn Hula Bowl Outstanding Lineman honors in 1964?

12. Who was the Ducks' All-American safety drafted by Carolina in the 1995 NFL Draft?

13. Who was the Oregon All-American DB who was the Defensive MVP of the 1992 Independence Bowl with two fumble recoveries and an interception in the Ducks' 39-35 loss to Wake Forest?

14. Who was the Oregon All-American DB who was the Defensive MVP of the 1989 Independence Bowl with two interceptions in the Ducks' 27-24 win over Tulsa?

15. Who was the last Oregon player with three interceptions in a game?

16. Which UO defender is the only one with 200+ tackles in a season (1969)?

17. Which two Ducks share the team record with 13 quarterback sacks in a season?

18. Tom Graham holds the school career tackles record with 433 from 1969-71. Since 2000, who has the most?

19. Which defender has the most career tackles for a loss?

20. Who owns the career record for most passes broken up?

21. Since 1990, who has the most career interceptions?

22. Who is the only player to lead the Ducks in tackles three consecutive seasons?

23. Which "Duck" walked on, then led the team in tackles in 2001 before playing six seasons in the NFL?

24. Which Oregon All-American DB, who had his career cut short due to a severe neck injury in his rookie NFL season of 1968, sued the NFL, leading to changes in the NFL Draft?

25. Which Oregon LB holds the school record for most tackles in a bowl game: 17, in the 2002 Seattle Bowl?

Short Yardage Crossword

Solution on page 151.

Across

1. Eugene Police blotter letters
4. Cow chow
7. Ducks Special Teams captain in 2007-08, Patrick ___
9. UO campus shade tree
10. Plumber's snake
11. Heisman Trophy Award Dinner mo.
12. Skis and kayak car rack name
13. Young cookie sellers org.
14. Commemorative marker
16. Have a Track Town Pizza
18. Main artery
21. Go downhill at Mount Hood Meadows
22. Wide, like shoulders
23. Break a Commandment
24. Ducks Special Teams Player of the Year in 2003 who made *USA Today*'s "NFL All-Joe Team" in '05
25. Opposite of WSW
26. Evensen has two

Down

1. Fountain of Youth Florida home: St. ___
2. Took a knee on the sideline
3. Prepared to consent
4. Fences made of shrubs
5. Ninkasi Brewing Co. brews
6. Village People hit played at most stadiums
7. U. of Arizona athlete, briefly
8. "Say what?"
15. *Two Women* Oscar winner, Sophia ___
16. Latin 101 verb
17. Similar (to)
19. ___ chi (martial art)
20. *The Register-Guard* revenue source

After solving the crossword puzzle, use the letters in the grid to answer the additional clue. Transfer the letters in numbered boxes to the corresponding blanks below. (Or answer the additional clue first to help you solve the crossword puzzle.)

Kickers' shoes

___ ___ ___ ___ ___ ___
7 15 26 5 19 21

Chapter 8

Special Teams

The Ducks' Cliff Harris was a consensus all-American punt returner in 2010, averaging 18.8 yards per return and running back four punts for touchdowns.

Add punter Jackson Rice's 42.3 punting average, Josh Huff's 24.7 yards per kickoff return and Rob Beard making 10-of-13 field goal attempts and Oregon was outstanding on special teams in 2010.

Through the years, the Ducks have been led by kickers Jared Siegel (49 field goals from 2001-04), Gregg McCallum (45 field goals from 1989-91), Tommy Thompson (37 field goals from 1990-93) and Joshua Smith (36 field from 1995-97).

Top punters in Oregon history include Mike Preacher (42.9-yard average from 1984-86), Len Isberg (42.8 average in 1940), Josh Syria (42.0 average in 2007-08), Kurtis Doerr (41.2 average in 1999-2000) and Josh Bidwell (40.8 average from 1995-98).

Top kick returners are Woodley Lewis (34.1-yard average from 1948-49), Jonathan Stewart (28.7 average from 2005-07), Michael McClellan (28.1 yard average from 1988-90), Chris Oldham (27.9 average from 1987-89) and Pat Johnson (27.4 average from 1994-97).

The top punt returners include Walter Thurmond III (15.0-yard average from 2006-09), Cliff Hicks (14.7 average from 1985-87), Jake Leicht (14.2 average from 1945-47), Jim Shanley (14.0 average from 1955-57) and Leroy Phelps (13.4 average from 1955-57).

Besides the specialists, the Pac-10 honors the players who cover kicks and block for returners. In 2010, the Ducks' Bryson Littlejohn was chosen to the second-team all-conference squad for his contributions to the various special teams.

Special Teams Crossword
Solution on page 152.

Across

1. UO punt returner Cliff (1985-87) or punter Kevin (1982-83)
6. Tree common near the Rose Bowl
10. No. 1 in the football poll
14. French farewell
15. Training room balm ingredient
16. Red Barn Natural Grocery fruit
17. Old computer-telephone hook-up
18. Safecracker
19. Whodunit board game
20. Defense acronym
22. Inquiring
24. ___ and outs
27. Star, like a Ducks All-American
30. Bit of color
31. Warty hopper
33. Mt. Mazama flow
34. Anaheim baseball player
35. Red Cross supply
37. Distinctive flair
38. In ___ of (replacing)
39. 3rd-___-7
40. Time out after a crushing hit?
44. Building additions
45. Vote John Kitzhaber back into office
47. Bryson Littlejohn's astrological ram sign
51. Cornerstone Cafe item: tuna ___
54. Oregon State Capitol feature
55. Kidney-related
56. Meddle
58. Early hour
59. Country of Eugene's sister city, Irkutsk
61. Fizzy drink at the concession stand
63. Eugene Symphony woodwind
64. Like most of UO's campus streets
67. Defeat
71. Scream for the Ducks
72. Mine finds
73. Euripides play lady
74. Extra point kicks on the scoreboard
75. "Hey, over here!"
76. Ducks kick returner from 1979-82 whose sister starred in the TV hit *Miami Vice*

Down

1. Honey Baked ___
2. Weddings on Call chapel vow (2 wds.)
3. El ___ (Spanish hero)
4. Astute
5. Poison plant
6. Bribe
7. Cornucopia brewed drink
8. Captain's journal
9. Start of something big?
10. Hold the football firmly (2 wds.)
11. Looking at amorously
12. Dive play into the center of the line
13. Connected on 49-of-69 FG from 2001-04
21. Business card abbr.
23. Lineman's ready position
24. "___ show time!"
25. Christmas carol
26. Bombay Palace Restaurant wrap

28. K who scored on a 2-pt. conversion in the 2007 Sun Bowl
29. Hairstyle of UO running backs coach Gary Campbell
32. Expected
36. Breakfast cereal
39. "___ for the poor"
41. Getting on in years
42. Cat call
43. Wile E. Coyote's supply company
46. Kicker's prop
47. Ducks punter in 2001-02 after transferring from Pasadena City College
48. The Embers' pastrami sandwich
49. Nike shoe part
50. UO art students' stands
52. Migratory grasshoppers
53. Also
57. Read a putt: ___ bob
60. On the peak of
62. Mimicker
65. Mins. and mins.
66. Hi-___ monitor
68. Tokyo, formerly
69. Just out
70. Former Ducks QB, ___ Fouts

Fill the Grid

It's your turn to be a crossword puzzle constructor. Using the name LEE in the diagonal (in honor of the Ducks kicker in 1982, Todd Lee), complete the grid with three three-letter words (or names or abbreviations common in crossword puzzles) going across that also make three three-letter words (or names or abbreviations) going down. There are several possible solutions. If you need help, here's a hint: The six letters we used for our solution are A-E-E-K-W-Y.

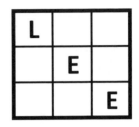

Now try one a bit tougher. Using the name OTTO in the diagonal (in honor of Dean Otto, the Ducks kicker who booted a 53-yard field goal in 1985), complete the grid with four four-letter words (or names or abbreviations common in crossword puzzles) going across that also make four four-letter words (or names or abbreviations) going down. There are a few possible solutions. If you need help, here's a hint: The 12 letters we used for our solution are A-E-H-I-I-L-O-O-R-S-U-Z.

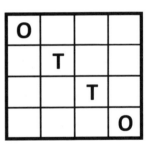

Solutions on page 153.

Special Teams Word Search

Solution on page 153.

```
H   I   C   K   S   V   C   D   D   L   F   L   I   N   T
O   X   Z   Y   P   D   G   R   E   B   S   I   O   D   N
W   X   S   Y   R   I   A   L   F   T   P   S   G   E   E
R   J   R   R   E   H   C   A   E   R   P   M   H   N   D
Y   J   M   C   C   A   L   L   U   M   A   S   U   N   L
Y   O   U   N   G   V   L   O   O   R   I   N   O   I   E
A   L   A   L   E   I   C   H   T   L   F   M   K   S   B
W   L   R   P   F   L   T   I   G   Y   R   I   C   E   O
B   Y   R   D   Z   L   N   N   E   U   T   A   V   B   L
I   M   O   R   B   E   E   L   H   X   D   E   E   M   G
D   O   Y   A   Z   G   N   T   J   O   N   E   S   E   C
W   U   O   E   B   A   W   H   C   S   D   D   I   C   Q
E   R   L   B   H   S   P   L   E   H   P   G   K   H   X
L   N   K   S   I   L   K   N   D   O   E   L   C   A   M
L   E   G   E   I   S   D   O   E   R   R   R   J   M   R
```

ARROYO	FLETCHER	LEICHT	SCHWABE
BEARD	FLINT	MACLEOD	SHANLEY
BELDEN	FRANKEL	MARTINEZ	SIEGEL
BIDWELL	GEIGER	MCCALLUM	SYRIA
BLANCHARD	HICKS	MECHAM	THOMPSON
DENNIS	HOWRY	OBEE	THURMOND
DOERR	ISBERG	PHELPS	VILLEGAS
ENGLISH	JOLLYMOUR	PREACHER	WOODFILL
EVENSEN	JONES	RICE	YOUNG

Oldham Sudoku

Use logic to fill in the boxes so every row, column and 2 x 3 box contains the letters O-L-D-H-A-M, in honor of Ducks kick returner Chris Oldham. As an added twist, the shaded areas also will contain the letters O-L-D-H-A-M. Solution on page 151.

	A		M	L	
		H			O
D			H	M	
	L	M			D
A			L		
	H	L		O	

Riley Showalter Sudoku

Use logic to fill in the grid below so that every row, column and 3 x 3 box contains the letters S-H-O-W-A-L-T-E-R, in honor of Riley Showalter, the Ducks' walk-on who earned three letters from 2007-09 as a Special Teams member and back-up linebacker. Solution on page 153.

	S				O	H		
	L						A	E
H		A	R			T		
T				S		O		
			W		L			
		H		R				S
		R			A	L		H
A	O						S	
		E	T				W	

Special Teams Trivia
Answers on page 152.

1. Who was the freshman running back in 2005 who led the nation in average kickoff return yardage?

2. Nathan Villegas kicked a game-tying field goal with 30 seconds remaining vs. USC in 1999, but was injured during the celebration. Who booted the winning field goal in the third overtime?

3. Besides Woody Lewis' record 102-yard kickoff return in 1949, who is the other UO player with a 100-yard return? Hint: He did it in 2009.

4. Which Ducks defensive lineman holds the school record with seven blocked kicks?

5. Which UO special teams player returned a punt 81 yards in 2001, but didn't score?

6. Who kicked the longest field goal in Oregon history?

7. Who made the most field goals for the Ducks in a season?

8. Which kicker went a perfect 8-for-8 in field goals in a season?

9. Who had the highest punting average in a season for the Ducks (46.0 in 1998)?

10. Who has the highest career field goal percentage for UO?

11. Which Oregon punter has the highest career punting average?

12. Cliff Harris has returned 29 punts in his career for an average of 18.8 yards per return. Besides Harris, which Ducks returner has the highest punt return average for a career (minimum of 10 returns)?

13. Who has the highest kickoff return average for a career?

14. Who punted a school record 12 times at UCLA in 2007?

15. Who returned a school record nine kickoffs at Stanford in 2009?

16. Who made the most extra-point kicks without a miss in his UO career?

17. Paul Martinez holds the Oregon record for most field goals made in a game (vs. Montana in 2005). How many did he make?

18. Jared Siegel holds the Oregon record for most consecutive field goals made. How many did he make in a row?

19. When was the last time the Ducks scored on a blocked punt?

20. Kurtis Doerr holds the school record for the longest punt. How far did his punt go?

21. Who was the long snapper for most of the 2010?

22. Who was the holder for most of the 2010 season?

23. Who was the last player to double up as the Ducks' field goal kicker and punter on a full-time basis?

24. Which former Ducks starting QB punted in the NFL for the Giants, Saints and Buccaneers?

25. Which former Oregon player was a punter in the 2006 Pro Bowl and has written an autobiography, *When It's Fourth And Long*?

Short Yardage Crossword

Solution on page 154.

Across

1. Ducks head coach from 1974-76 who later led Montana to a Div. I-AA national championship
5. Neighbor of a Vietnamese
8. Stocking color
9. Santa's little helper
10. ___ out (declined)
11. In shape
12. Keep the QB from being sacked
14. Fleshy fruit
15. Size up
18. Pertaining to the mouth
20. Spring football mo.
22. Be nuts about the Ducks
23. Opening between blockers
24. Photographer's camera part
25. UO baseball bat wood
26. Ducks head coach from 1967-71 who was born in the city of Oregon, Wisconsin

Down

1. Copy, for short
2. Body types: ___, Mesomorph and Endomorph
3. Narrow mountain ridges
4. Type of tourist ranch
5. Undisturbed (2 wds.)
6. *Sports Illustrated*'s 1974 Sportsman of the Year
7. Frequently, in verse
10. Foe: Abbr.
13. Less refined
16. Ankle bones
17. Bard's "before" at the Oregon Shakespeare Festival
19. Baby elephant at the Oregon Zoo
20. ___ Khan
21. Mas' mates

After solving the crossword puzzle, use the letters in the grid to answer the additional clue. Transfer the letters in numbered boxes to the corresponding blanks below. (Or answer the additional clue first to help you solve the crossword puzzle.)

Column heading for coach's lifetime record

___ ___ ___ ___ ___ ___
19 6 15 2 17 1

Chapter 9

Coaches

The Ducks' Chip Kelly was the National Coach the Year in 2010 and has compiled a record of 22-4 in his first two years as a college head coach.

The New Hampshire native came to Eugene in 2007 as UO's offensive coordinator. After two years of record-breaking performances, he was promoted to his first head coaching position.

Kelly graduated from the University of New Hampshire in 1990 and got his start in coaching at Columbia. After two seasons, he returned to his alma mater as running backs coach. In 1993 he was named defensive coordinator at Johns Hopkins University.

After a year at Johns Hopkins, Kelly again returned to UNH. He was the running backs coach for three seasons, the offensive line coach for two years, then was the school's offensive coordinator from 1999-2006.

Under Kelly, New Hampshire utilized the spread offense and set numerous school records. That success led to Kelly's hiring by Oregon.

"I've always felt that Oregon was one of the elite football programs in the country," Kelly said. "We will always strive to be in the top part of the college football landscape. Year in and year out, I want people to talk consistently about Oregon with the top football programs in the country."

The winningest coach in Oregon history is Mike Bellotti, who won 116 games in 14 seasons from 1995-2008. Next on the list is Rich Brooks, with 91 victories in 18 seasons from 1977-94.

Percy Benson (1895) has the best lifetime winning percentage (100.0, 4-0), followed by Kelly (.846), Gordon Frost (.833 in 1907) and C.W. Spears (.737 from 1930-31).

Coaching Boxes

Place the names of these 17 UO head coaches into the grid, one name for each row and no more than one letter per box, so that the highlighted column reading down spells out a phrase that is related to the puzzle theme. We've given you hints on where some of the names go by putting all of the Ds, Us, Cs, Ks and Ss in place. You must use all of the names, but not all the boxes will have a letter in them. Our solution on page 155.

Coaches:

- AIKEN
- BELLOTTI
- BROOKS
- CHURCH
- DOLPH
- ENRIGHT
- FREI
- FRICK
- FROST
- KELLY
- MCEWAN
- OLIVER
- READ
- SHORTS
- SMITH
- SPEARS
- YOUNG

1	2	3	4	5	6	7	8	9
		S					S	
		U						
						K	S	
		K						
	S					S		
				D				
				C				
					D			
				C	K			
			C		U		C	
			K					
				S				

Chip Kelly Wordsmith

Using the letters C-H-I-P-K-E-L-L-Y, how many words of four or more letters can you make? We found 31 fairly common words (plus 30 not so common ones that are acceptable in a tournament game of SCRABBLE). Proper nouns, foreign words and abbreviations don't count. If you can find 25 or more words in 25 minutes, you're an All-American Wordsmith. Solution on page 154.

Coaches Crossword

Solution on page 154.

Across

1. Highlander
5. Sheltered from the wind
9. In the sack
13. Angel's headwear
14. Possible nickname for Steve Young or Kenny Stabler
16. Building block at the Children's Museum
17. Made a touchdown?
18. Baseball bat making tool
19. Blackthorn fruit
20. Washington, to Washington State
22. Representative sign
24. Oregon Zoo spotted wildcat
26. UO basketball career scoring leader, Ron ___
27. Peculiar
30. Neither's partner
31. Nitwit
34. Food and drink of the Gods
36. Dipping chocolate or cheese at The Vintage (Var.)
37. 4:1, e.g.
38. Central points
41. First coach in Pac-10 history to win an outright conference title in his first season
44. Talk like Daffy Duck
45. Asinine
47. Explode at the ref (2 wds.)
49. Climb in the weekly football polls (2 wds.)
51. Needle case
52. Dorm room fixture
55. Eugene Airport posting: Abbr.
56. Make fun of
58. Hunger
60. 5th Ave. restaurant: Cafe Lucky ___
63. Dart through the hole
64. Scent
66. Come from behind
69. Puff
70. Pine Mountain Observatory sighting
71. Clear the locker room chalkboard
72. Aloha Bowl stringed instruments
73. Term paper footnote abbr.
74. They're tight, split and defensive
75. "Hey, over here!"

Down

1. Mrs. Ozzy Osbourne
2. Spotted cat
3. Coach "Tex"
4. Add up
5. Apiece, in scores
6. Grazing area
7. New newts
8. Gas additive
9. *The Sun ___ Rises*
10. Winningest Ducks coach
11. Freudian topic in Psych 101
12. Anonymous John
15. Land on the Red Sea
21. New Mexico athlete
23. "Cold one" at a campus bar
25. Honky-___
28. Speaker's platform
29. Plummet in the football polls
32. Poem of praise

33. Swell
35. University farms new born
36. Monetary penalty
38. Can the coach
39. "Step ___!" (2 wds.)
40. Former coach's name on the UO athletic center
42. Windermere Real Estate offering
43. Y'all (Informal)
46. Continental money
48. Partner of starts
50. San Diego baseball player
52. National Coach of the Year in 1994 after leading UO to the Rose Bowl
53. Elicits
54. Can't stand, like Washington fans
57. Menacing look from a linebacker
59. Misbehave on the sideline (2 wds.)
61. Face-to-face exam
62. Distinctive flair
64. "We're number ___!"
65. Period, in Web addresses
67. It was dropped in the '60s
68. "Indeed!"

Cryptic Quote

The Cryptic Quote is a substitution cipher in which one letter stands for another. If you think that A equals Z, it will equal Z throughout the puzzle. Solve this Cryptic Quote from UO Coach Chip Kelly. Solution on page 156.

" J V   S Y G V   Y K

Y L L Y U N   N D K I X V L

P W Q N   L S V   C V L - C Q .

J V ' W V   C Q D K C   L Q

L W E   L Q   R W V X X Z W V

E Q Z   D K   Y X   N Y K E

J Y E X   Y X   J V   U Y K ,

P W Q N   L S V   L V N R Q

J V   R B Y E   Y L   L Q

L S V   P Q W N Y L D Q K X

J V   W Z K . "

Coaches Word Search
Answer on page 155.

```
K  C  R  C  N  U  A  I  K  E  N  I  Z  M  G
E  H  E  L  F  R  I  C  H  M  C  E  W  A  N
L  U  A  L  I  O  T  T  I  E  R  F  N  D  U
L  R  D  E  A  G  R  E  A  T  W  O  O  D  O
Y  C  R  B  R  E  N  R  O  B  S  O  T  O  Y
W  H  F  P  M  U  L  L  E  P  F  S  G  C  D
W  R  O  M  Y  H  T  I  M  S  B  R  N  K  O
A  E  R  A  D  C  L  I  F  F  E  A  I  T  L
R  V  B  C  C  V  S  P  T  B  N  E  T  H  P
R  I  E  S  T  R  O  H  S  T  S  P  N  G  H
E  L  S  N  K  C  I  R  F  N  O  S  U  I  T
N  O  S  I  L  L  A  C  A  G  N  L  H  R  O
R  A  V  O  N  A  S  A  C  T  M  O  L  N  C
A  M  A  H  K  N  I  P  T  K  E  D  Z  E  B
W  N  G  W  T  S  O  R  F  S  K  O  O  R  B
```

AIKEN	CHURCH	HUNTINGTON	RADCLIFFE
ALIOTTI	DOLPH	KAARSBERG	READ
BELLOTTI	ENRIGHT	KELLY	SHORTS
BENSON	FORBES	MADDOCK	SIMPSON
BEZDEK	FREI	MCEWAN	SMITH
BROOKS	FRICK	OLIVER	SPEARS
CALLISON	FROST	OSBORNE	WARNER
CAMPBELL	GREATWOOD	PELLUM	WARREN
CASANOVA	HELFRICH	PINKHAM	YOUNG

John McKay Sudoku

Use logic to fill in the grid below so that every row, column and 3 x 3 box contains the letters J-O-H-N-M-C-K-A-Y, in honor of John McKay, who played for the Ducks (1948-49) and was an assistant coach with the Ducks (1950-58) before embarking on a Hall of Fame career as the head coach of USC and the Tampa Bay Buccaneers. Solution on page 156.

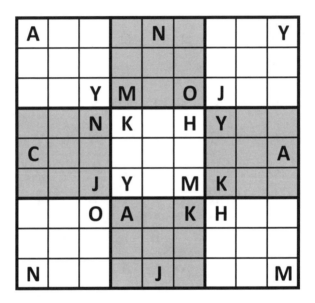

Who Am I? Sudoku

Use logic to fill in the boxes so every row, column and 2 x 3 box contains the letters of a memorable UO head coach. (Hint: He coached the Ducks for six seasons.) When completed, the row indicated by the arrow will spell out the name correctly. Solution on page 154.

Coaches Trivia
Answers on page 156.

1. Who was the first person to play and coach for the same school in the Rose Bowl?

2. Besides Oregon, where was Mike Bellotti a college head coach?

3. Who was the first UO coach to win 10 games in a season?

4. Who was the coach of the Ducks when they played in the Rose Bowl following the 1994 season?

5. Which NFL team did Rich Brooks coach after leaving UO?

6. Where did Rich Brooks play college football?

7. Which other Oregon school did Don Read coach before and after coaching UO?

8. Which former UO head coach was the coach at Capistrano Valley High School in Mission Viejo, Calif., when future USC and NFL quarterback Todd Marinovich had one of the greatest high school seasons ever?

9. Which UO head coach was a teammate of Crazylegs Hirsch at Wisconsin in 1942?

10. Which Oregon head coach was told to fire his assistant coaches, among them future NFL head coaches John Robinson, George Seifert and Gunther Cunningham?

11. Which future UO head coach had a 97-yard punt as a player at Santa Clara University?

12. Which Oregon head coach is the school's Freshman of the Year Award named in honor of?

13. Who played in the Rose Bowl for Washington & Jefferson, then coached UO in the Cotton Bowl?

14. Who was the Oregon head coach who left his position in 1942 to join the Navy, then returned to his position after the war?

15. Who am I?
    * I played at Oregon from 1920-22.
    * I coached Medford High School to two state basketball championships.
    * I was the head coach of Oregon in 1933 when it went 9-1 and tied for the Pacific Coast Conference title.
    * My real name was Prince, but I was called Prink.

16. Which UO football head coach also coached the Oregon basketball and baseball teams, then was the head coach of the Cleveland Rams in the NFL and the manager of the Pittsburgh Pirates in the Major Leagues?

17. Which College Football Hall of Fame member and UO head coach was the head coach at the U.S. Military Academy before arriving in Eugene in 1926?

18. Who was the assistant basketball coach who took over Oregon's football team for a year during World War II and compiled a 2-6 record? Hint: He eventually became UO's head basketball coach.

19. Which UO head coach and College Football Hall of Fame member was an All-American guard at Dartmouth in 1914 and '15?

20. Which Oregon head coach became a medical doctor?

Chip Kelly Trivia
Answers on page 157.

1. Who did the Ducks beat to give Chip Kelly his first college head coaching win?

2. Which Pac-10 school was the only one to beat the Ducks in the 2009-10 seasons?

3. Where did Coach Kelly graduate from college?

4. Where did he get his first coaching job out of college?

5. Which three sports did "Chipper" Kelly play at Manchester, N.H., Central High School?

Short Yardage Crossword

Solution on page 157.

1	2	3				4	5	6
7			■			8		
9		■	10	11	12	■	13	
	■	14			15	■	
	■	16					■	
	■	17					■	
18	19	■	20			■	21	
22		23	■	■	24			
25								

Across

1. Having a blunt snout
7. Used to be
8. Darron Thomas' uniform number
9. Attached to
10. Dine late at Ron's Island Grill
13. Engage in
14. Sleeping disorder
16. UO athletes
17. Lowest deck on a ship
18. Word when viewed upside down is Spanish for yes
20. Kicker's prop
21. UO graduate deg.
22. Coll. in Ashland
24. Come out on top in the game
25. Links on a Web site, e.g.

Down

1. Newman's Fish Company catch
2. A Bobbsey twin
3. ___ vs. Them
4. Alternative to K on a baseball scorecard
5. Football lineman
6. Toiletry in a player's locker
10. Squirt
11. "I give up!"
12. Tea variety
14. *Much ___ About Nothing*
15. Egyptian snake
19. Sauce with sushi at Kabuki's
21. Combine
23. Ahead in the game
24. You and me

After solving the crossword puzzle, use the letters in the grid to answer the additional clue. Transfer the letters in numbered boxes to the corresponding blanks below. (Or answer the additional clue first to help you solve the crossword puzzle.)

UO graduate who produced the movies *Flashdance, Beverly Hills Cop, Top Gun, Crimson Tide* and *The Rock*, among others

___ ___ ___ ___ ___ ___ ___
10 18 21 12 1 18 2

Chapter 10

Overtime

The University of Oregon was established in 1872. The first building on campus was what is today known as Deady Hall, named in honor of Oregon's first federal judge, Matthew Deady.

Today, the public institution located in Eugene, has about 20,000 undergraduate students and an additional 4,000 graduate students. The University is organized into eight schools and colleges.

The City of Eugene is the second largest city in Oregon with a population of about 150,000. Known as "Emerald City" and "Track Town, U.S.A.," Eugene was the birthplace of the mega-corporation, Nike.

Eugene is named after Eugene F. Skinner, its founder in 1846. Skinner was a settler who established a farm in the area as well as a ferry service. Historians suggest that Skinner chose the site to establish a monopoly on the ferry service across the Willamette River.

Notable alumni from UO include Nike co-founders Bill Bowerman and Phil Knight, Golden State Warriors' principal owner Franklin Mieuli, New Orleans Saints general manager Mickey Loomis, Gucci chairman and CEO Robert Polet, co-founder of *Reader's Digest* Lila Bell Wallace, Wieden+Kennedy advertising agency co-founder Dan Wieden, Tony Award winner Jeff Whitty, author Ken Kesey, NBA executive Stu Jackson, former NBA guard Ron Lee, track star Mary Decker, track star Steve Prefontaine and track star Alberto Salazar.

Famous natives of Eugene include former NBA player and Boston Celtics executive Danny Ainge, former pro golfer Casey Martin, astronaut Stanley Love, science fiction writer David Bischoff and actress Rebecca Schaeffer.

Presidential Box

Starting anywhere in the box,
use adjacent letters—vertically,
horizontally or diagonally—to make
as many words as you can from
the letters in RICHARD LARIVIERE
(the president of the University of
Oregon). Words need to be three
or more letters and cannot use the
same letter cube more than once

R	I	C	H
A	R	D	L
A	R	I	V
I	E	R	E

per word. No proper nouns, hyphenated or foreign words and no
slang. We found about 40 "common" words, but there are a total
of 63 words that are in *The Official SCRABBLE Players Dictionary*.
Find 35 words in 30 minutes to earn induction into the Solving
Hall of Fame. List of words on page 157.

Missing D-U-C-K

Fill in the blanks with the letters D-U-C-K, once each, in any order, to form a fairly common seven-letter word in each line. Solution on page 157.

1. T R __ __ __ E __

2. __ H __ C __ E __

3. S __ N __ E __ __

4. B __ __ __ L E __

5. __ __ __ __ P I N

6. Q __ A __ __ E __

7. M __ __ P A __ __

8. __ A __ L __ E __

Autzen Sudoku

Use logic to fill in the boxes so every row, column and 2 x 3 box contains the letters A-U-T-Z-E-N, in honor of UO's Autzen Stadium. Solution on page 157.

T		A	U		N
Z		N	A		
		E	N		Z
N		Z	E		T

Overtime Crossword
Solution on page 158.

Across

1. Mouth off to opposing players
5. Comcast in Eugene: ___ TV
10. Truth or ___ (tailgate party game)
14. Clever offensive team tactic
15. OHSU School of Dentistry filling
16. U. of Miami mascot
17. Millions of years
18. Make amends for a fumble
19. Seductress
20. Riddle, Part 1
23. Taste of India wrap (Var.)
24. Conger Street Clock Museum numeral
25. Disobeyed an Oregon Zoo sign?
28. Mediterranean Sea island republic
32. Covet
34. Word said with a tongue depressor in your mouth
37. Exit the stadium
39. Graph line
40. Riddle, Part 2
44. Oregon Dunes bird
45. BYU's city
46. Mas' mates
47. Girders
50. Some Romanovs
52. St. Louis pro football player
53. Cousin of an ostrich
55. Bullwinkle, for one
59. Answer to riddle
63. Lacking sensation
66. Skirts in a UO ballet class
67. Kind of package from home
68. Term paper footnote abbr.
69. Former UO basketball coach, ___ Kent
70. Kind of proportions
71. Declare untrue to the ref
72. UO Marching Band's former footwear
73. Falling out

Down

1. Gushes, like a Cascade volcano
2. Ducks' 1997 bowl game
3. Oregon Coast whale finder
4. Solar ___
5. Noli Italian Cafe "bye"
6. Not pro
7. Oregon legislative group
8. Hawaiian island
9. Lens cover?
10. Eugene Opera prima donna
11. UO's Steve Jones' pro hoop league
12. McArthur Court backboard attachment
13. Psychic power
21. Distributed cards at Three Rivers Casino
22. Tell it like it isn't
25. Play matchmaker
26. Ducks' golf star, ___ Omlid
27. Classroom stations
29. Malachi Lewis' astrological sign
30. PK Park field covering
31. Turn aside
33. Down in the dumps after a loss
34. Buzzing, like Autzen Stadium on game day
35. Tiny organism

36. MC Hammer pants
38. Psych 101 topics
41. Genetic letters
42. Lab eggs
43. Former Oregon Secretary of State, ___ Paulus
48. Kitten's cry
49. Inflicts a heavy blow
51. UO women's sport
54. Take over
56. Cousin of a giraffe

57. Printing flourish
58. Construct, like Matthew Knight Arena
59. With competence
60. Altamont's ___ Park
61. Throw in the towel
62. Operates
63. Former UO basketball star, ___ Fowler
64. Western Indian
65. Type of pass defense, briefly

Quote Pickup

The letters in each vertical column go into the squares directly above them, but not necessarily in the order they appear. The black squares indicate the end of a word. When you have placed all the letters in their correct positions, you will have a quotation reading from left to right, row by row. The quote is from Doug Franz of KTAR Radio in Phoenix. Answer is on page 157.

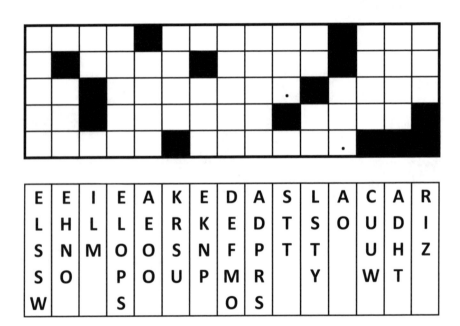

One and Only One

Hidden in the grid is one and only one complete NIKE. It might run up, down, sideways or diagonally. See if you can find it. Solution on page 158.

```
N K I E I N N K E I N I K I N
I K E N K I E N I K K I N E I
K E I N I E K I I K N I K N K
N I K K E I N K K E N E K N I
N I K K N N I K I N K I N K E
I K E N I K I K E N I K K E I
N K I E E E K K K I I I N N N
I N K E N K K I I N I I K I I
K I I N K E N K I E K N E K N
I N K E K I K E E E K I E I E
N E K E K K I E E N K I I K N
I E K K E N N E I I K E K I K
K N I N N E N N E N I N I E I
N E K I I N K E I N N K E N I
I N I E I K E I K E I N K I N
```

Chip Kelly

Ducks TXT

Use your cell phone keypad to help decode the last names of these Oregon players on the 2010 squad. In the example 7423, the 7 could be P, Q, R or S; the 4 could be G, H or I; the 2 could be A, B or C; and the 3 could be D, E or F. The player's name found in that text is R-I-C-E, Jackson Rice, the punter for the Ducks. Now try these. Answers on page 158.

1. 62345
2. 32847
3. 75327268
4. 465637
5. 729746437
6. 5225766
7. 2247
8. 7693
9. 227637
10. 53947

Across & Down Words

There are 11 football terms and a UO football phrase in the diagram. Taking one letter from each box across the top row, find a 4-letter football term. Cross off the letters as you use them. Do the same for the other six rows. Then take one of the remaining letters from each box and go down the first column to find a 7-letter football term. Cross off those letters. Do the same for the other three columns. The remaining letters, one per box, will reveal the phrase, reading left to right, row by row. Solution on page 159.

Across

_____
_____
_____
_____
_____
_____

E	Q	D	E
R T	U U	G S	H K
A	E	A	I
N P	L U	E O	R Y
C	A	D	C
E E	G N	F O	N S
I	R	E	K
K P	S U	H N	O T
B	A	L	L
L M	E T	N T	O O
E	E	A	D
F T	H L	E S	F G
D	A	E	F
P U	C R	K S	S S

Down

_____
_____
_____

Phrase

_____

Quote Box

Starting with the large P in the shaded box below, move one square up, down, left or right (but not diagonally) and continue to move that way to spell out a quote about Autzen Stadium from longtime ABC sportscaster Keith Jackson. The quote runs continuously by using each letter exactly once. Solution on page 159.

U	I	D	A	T	S	T
M	T	H	E	H	I	S
I	N	T	E	N	S	E
R	E	**P**	L	A	T	D
S	A	R	P	E	O	U
Q	Y	D	T	H	R	O
U	E	I	F	O	Y	L
A	R	T	S	T	H	E

Fourth Down

From this list of five words, determine which word doesn't have what the other four do. (Hint: There is a UO connection.) Answer on page 159.

BREEDER

MIDWESTERN

PIONEER

PLUNGER

RASPBERRY

Overtime Trivia
Answers on page 160.

1. Who was the halfback/defensive tackle who led Oregon to its only Rose Bowl win on Jan. 1, 1917, then was on the winning team at the Rose Bowl again a year later as a member of the Mare Island Marines?

2. Which former Ducks player was an announcer on *Monday Night Football*?

3. Which former UO quarterback played himself in the football comedy *The Waterboy*?

4. Which Oregon star is the only player to lead the conference in scoring twice from two different positions?

5. Who are the two Ducks to earn All-America honors on the field and in the classroom?

6. Which Oregon back finished second in the 1962 NCAA 120-yard high hurdles?

7. Which UO quarterback turned down a lucrative contract from MLB's New York Yankees to play in the NFL?

8. Who is the only Oregon player to lead the team in rushing, receiving and scoring for a season (but not the same season)?

9. Which DB was the first Oregon player to leave campus early to enter the NFL Draft in 1997?

10. The Ducks have had one letterman whose surname begins with the letter Q. Who is he?

11. Name the five former Oregon Ducks who played in the 1985 Super Bowl with the San Francisco 49ers.

12. Which former UO quarterback is the longtime analyst on Oregon game broadcasts?

13. Who receives the Gordon E. Wilson Award, named in honor of the former letterman?

14. Which Big Ten school is Oregon 0-8 all-time, UO's worst record against any opponent?

15. Who is Autzen Stadium named after?

16. Who is Autzen Stadium's playing surface named in honor of?

17. The Ducks played in front of 102,035 fans at Tennessee in 2010. Where did the Ducks play in front of 109,733 fans in 2007?

18. Which Washington State RB holds the Autzen Stadium record of 357 rushing yards in a game?

19. Where was Rob Mullens the athletics director before becoming the A.D. at UO?

20. Who is the longtime radio voice of Ducks football and basketball games?

21. Besides Eugene and Corvallis, where have UO-Oregon State games been played?

22. What is the name of the Civil War trophy?

23. The name "Civil War" was first referenced in 1929 and commonly used since 1937. What was the series called before that?

24. The only year both Oregon (5th) and Oregon State (8th) were ranked in the Top 10 at the time of the game was 2000. Who won the game?

25. Oregon and Oregon State have played 114 times. Which other Pac-10 rivalry has played the same number of games?

Stefanick Sudoku

Use logic to fill in the grid below so that every row, column and 3 x 3 box contains the letters S-T-E-F-A-N-I-C-K, in honor of Jeff Stefanick, an offensive tackle from 1984-87 and co-captain of the 1987 team. That 1987 squad was the first in UO history to defeat both Washington and Oregon State in Eugene in the same season. Solution on page 159.

E		F			K			
	T			N				I
				T		F		
	E		T					K
		K				T		
C				F		N		
	N		E					
K			S			A		
			K		S		C	

Norm Van Brocklin

Answers

Chapter 1

Wilcox Sudoku (from page 11)

O	I	W	C	X	L
C	L	X	I	O	W
W	O	L	X	I	C
X	C	I	W	L	O
L	X	C	O	W	I
I	W	O	L	C	X

History Short Yardage (from page 4)

Additional Clue: FIESTA

F	O	U	T	S		J	A	R
I	N	S	E	T		U	M	P
T	E	A	S	E		D	I	M
			T	W	E	E	T	
	I	C	E		M	A	Y	
	C	A	R	I	B			
F	I	R		C	R	U	M	P
I	L	O		B	Y	F	A	R
G	Y	M		M	O	O	R	E

History Crossword (from page 6)

Duck Soup (from page 8)

All-Americans: COTA, MOLDEN, MOORE, REED, RENFRO, VAN BROCKLIN; 2010
Players: BEARD, HARRIS, JAMES, MATTHEWS, THOMAS; Coaches: BELLOTTI, BROOKS,
CASANOVA, READ; Bowl Games: FIESTA, ROSE, SUN; Colors: GREEN, YELLOW;
Athletics Director: MULLENS.
Hidden Phrase: OREGON, OUR ALMA MATER, WE WILL GUARD THEE ON AND ON.
(The first line of the UO fight song, "Mighty Oregon.")

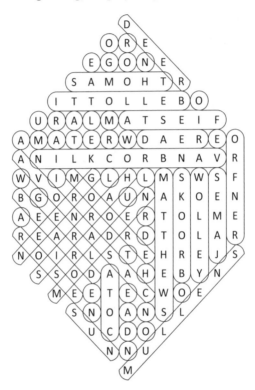

Bowl Game Categories (from page 10)

Defensive Players: BYRD, OLDHAM, WHEATON, LONG, GOLDSMITH, AGYEMAN,
MORETTI, EDWARDS; Offensive Players: BARNES, O'NEIL, WHITTLE, LUCAS, GLASS,
AKERMAN, MILLER, ELLIOTT; Football Terms: BLOCK, OFFSIDES, WIDE RECEIVER,
LATERAL, GOAL LINE, AUDIBLE, MOTION, END ZONE; Oregon Cities: BEAVERTON,
ONTARIO, WOODBURN, LEBANON, GRESHAN, ALBANY, MEDFORD, EUGENE.

History Trivia (from pages 13)

1. Jake Leicht.
2. The Huntingtons, Shy and Hollis.
3. Joey Harrington, following by 2) Dennis Dixon, 3) Haloti Ngata, 4) Jonathan
   Stewart, 5) Nick Reed, 6) Max Unger, 7) Kellen Clemens, 8) Keenan Howry, 9)
   Samie Parker, and 10) Patrick Chung.

4. More than; the Ducks had 720 yards.
5. Nevada (1999) and New Mexico (2010).
6. 65.
7. The last five games of 2001 and the first six games of 2002.
8. 2004 (5-6).
9. 2000 (10-2).
10. 1957.
11. Jordan Holmes, Jeremiah Masoli, Walter Thurmond III and Will Tukuafu.
12. 1982 (a 13-13 tie). The other time the two schools played was 1976 (ND 41, UO 0).
13. Oregon has beaten Oregon State 58 times (with 46 losses and 10 ties).
14. Nov. 30, 1948 (9th).
15. Spokane, Wash.
16. 1967.
17. Hayward Field.
18. Joey Harrington, on Jan. 1, 2002.
19. Kenny Rowe.
20. Southern Methodist, 21-14.
21. Fresno State; the Ducks won, 30-27.
22. Oregon State, 38-31, in 2007.
23. Larry Hill. The game ended in a 21-21 tie.
24. Lu Bain, Bob Berry, Larry Hill and Mel Renfro.
25. 1936.

Who Am I? Sudoku (from page 11)

Dick DAUGHERTY, who was an offensive lineman/linebacker for the Ducks in 1950, then won an NFL title with the Los Angeles Rams the following season. He played six years in the NFL, earning all-pro accolades in 1957.

Y	G	T	U	R	A	H	D	E
A	U	H	Y	E	D	G	R	T
E	R	D	H	T	G	U	Y	A
G	T	Y	R	A	U	D	E	H
D	A	U	G	H	E	R	T	Y
H	E	R	D	Y	T	A	U	G
T	H	G	E	U	R	Y	A	D
U	Y	A	T	D	H	E	G	R
R	D	E	A	G	Y	T	H	U

Chapter 2

Alston Sudoku (from page 26)

T	A	O	S	L	N
L	N	S	T	A	O
O	T	A	L	N	S
N	S	L	O	T	A
A	O	T	N	S	L
S	L	N	A	O	T

2010 Team Short Yardage (from page 16)

Additional Clue: ASPER

			R	O	W	E		
		T	R	A	L	A	L	A
S	W	O	R	D	S	M	A	N
T	O	T	E	M		S	H	E
I			R	A	P			W
F	E	D		S	L	A	P	S
F	R	O	N	T	A	L	L	Y
	G	R	E	E	N	L	Y	
	Y	O	R	K				

All Mixed Up (from page 18)

Offense: 1. PAULSON; 2. THRAN; 3. KAISER; 4. THOMAS; 5. JAMES; 6. TUINEI; 7. YORK; 8. ASPER; 9. ALSTON; 10. WEEMS.

Defense: 1. BOYETT; 2. MATTHEWS; 3. GILDON; 4. KADDU; 5. CLARK; 6. TURNER; 7. JOHNSON; 8. PEPPARS; 9. HARRIS; 10. LITTLEJOHN.

2010 Team Crossword (from page 20)

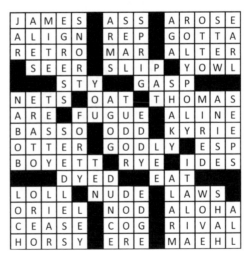

Top 25 Teams Word Search (from page 19)

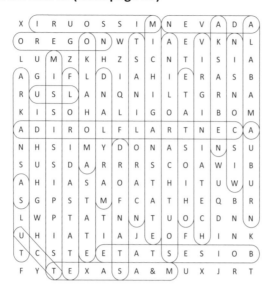

Golpashin Sudoku (from page 26)

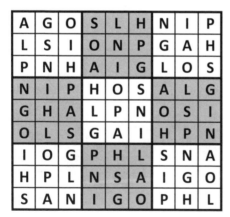

2010 Season Trivia (from pages 22)

1. Cam Newton of Auburn won the award and Stanford's Andrew Luck was second.
2. Cliff Harris. His six interceptions tied for fourth in the nation.
3. LaMichael James with 144 points on 24 touchdowns.
4. The yellow T-shirts sported the slogan "Quack Out Loud."
5. Senior Casey Matthews and freshman Boseko Lokombo.
6. Running back LaMichael James and tight end David Paulson.
7. From 1998-2001, the Ducks won 38 games.

8. DT Brandon Bair, CB Talmadge Jackson III, WR Jeff Maehl, LB Spencer Paysinger and DE Kenny Rowe.
9. Portland State.
10. He had 257 yards against Stanford, the second highest total in school history.
11. Demetrius Williams with 1,059 yards in 2005.
12. Wide receiver Josh Huff.
13. New Mexico and Portland State.
14. Kenjon Barner, who had all five TDs before halftime against New Mexico.
15. Cliff Harris.
16. Washington on Nov. 6.
17. Quarterback Darron Thomas, defensive end Terrell Turner and defensive tackle Zac Clark.
18. Casey Matthews.
19. Kenny Rowe.
20. Alejandro Maldonado, who punted three times (for a 36-yard average).
21. Kenjon Barner, who had six rushing TDs, two receiving TDs and one punt return TD.
22. A total of 1,280 combinations.
23. New Mexico and Tennessee.
24. Mark Helfrich.
25. TE Curtis White (Sheldon HS), DE Nick Musgrove (Churchill HS), WR Justin Hoffman (Churchill HS) and QB Dustin Haines (South Eugene HS).

(Phil) Knight Moves (from page 28)

18	59	50	1	48	15	22	
51	2	17	60	21		47	14
58	19	4	49	16	23		45
3	52	57	20	61	46	13	24
34	5	40	53	36	25	44	11
39	56	35	8	41	12	29	26
6	33	54	37	28	31	10	43
55	38	7	32	9	42	27	30

2010 Season Word Search (from page 29)

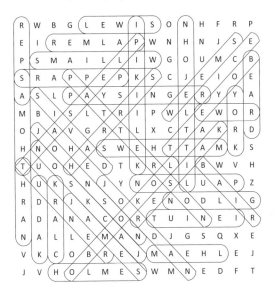

Chapter 3

Ogburn Sudoku (from page 34)

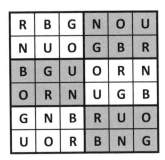

Quarterbacks Short Yardage (from page 30)

Additional Clue: BERRY

	P	A	M		C	H	I	
F	O	C	I		R	U	T	
E	L	A	N		T	R	I	M
E	L	I	O	T		R	N	A
L	I	B	R	A	R	I	E	S
E	N	E		M	A	C	R	O
Y	A	R	D		B	A	A	L
	T	R	Y		A	N	T	I
	E	Y	E		T	E	E	

Pick A Letter (from page 32)

1. SHAW; 2. FOUTS; 3. MILLER; 4. O'NEIL; 5. CLEMENS; 6. MASOLI; 7. DIXON; 8. MUSGRAVE; 9. FEELEY; 10. OGBURN.

Crossing Patterns (from page 35)

1.BOB BERRY; 2. JASON MAAS; 3. DENNIS DIXON; 4. AKILI SMITH; 5. CHRIS MILLER; 6. KELLEN CLEMENS.

Quarterbacks Crossword (from page 36)

Quarterbacks Word Search (from page 33)

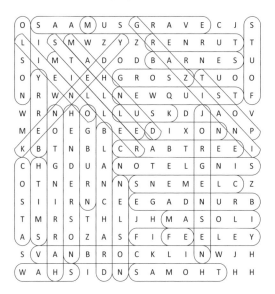

Dave Grosz Sudoku (from page 34)

V	A	S	D	G	O	Z	R	E
E	D	R	A	Z	V	S	G	O
O	G	Z	R	S	E	V	A	D
Z	S	G	E	O	A	R	D	V
A	E	D	V	R	Z	G	O	S
R	O	V	S	D	G	A	E	Z
D	V	A	Z	E	R	O	S	G
S	Z	O	G	A	D	E	V	R
G	R	E	O	V	S	D	Z	A

Quarterbacks Trivia (from page 38)

1. Jeremiah Masoli.
2. Dennis Dixon. He hit .176 in 74 at bats that summer.
3. Dan Fouts, with 2,390 yards in 1970.
4. Joey Harrington; the 1999 Sun Bowl, 2000 Holiday Bowl and 2002 Fiesta Bowl.
5. Joey Harrington with 108 from 1998-2001.
6. Chris Miller.
7. Bill Musgrave with 8.343 passing yards and 8,140 yards of total offense from 1987-90.
8. George Shaw, who was picked by the Baltimore Colts and played for four NFL teams in eight years, compiling a record of 11-16-2 as a starter.
9. Akili Smith.
10. Reggie Ogburn with 644 yards in 1979.
11. Jason Fife, who currently is in dental school after stints in the NFL and Arena Football League.
12. Bob Berry.
13. Norm Van Brocklin, who led the Philadelphia Eagles to the NFL title.
14. The University of Mississippi where he threw for 2,039 yards and ran for 544 yards in 2010.
15. Jeremiah Masoli, with 714 yards in 2008.
16. Kellen Clemens (2003-05), Joey Harrington (2000-01), Jason Maas (1997), Danny O'Neil (1991-94) and Mike Jorgensen (1982-83).
17. Danny O'Neil (1991-94), who played one season in the Arena Football League, then became a pastor in Eugene.
18. Kellen Clemens, who was the backup QB for the New York Jets in 2010.
19. Norv Turner, head coach of the NFL's Redskins, Raiders and Chargers, and June Junes, head coach of the NFL's Falcons and Chargers.
20. Tony Graziani and Ryan Perry-Smith.
21. Bill Musgrave, with 489 yards vs. BYU in 1989.
22. Danny O'Neil, with six TD passes vs. Stanford in 1994.

23. Jack Henderson.
24. Tom Blanchard, at Illinois.
25. Shy Huntington, who also intercepted three passes in the game.

Chapter 4

Who Am I? Sudoku (from page 51)
LeGarrette BLOUNT

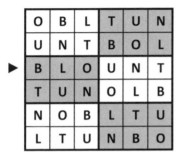

Running Backs Short Yardage (from page 42)
Additional Clue: JAMES

Ifs and Thens (from page 44)
DEREK LOVILLE

What's in a Name? (from page 49)
1. ONTERRIO SMITH; 2. SEAN BURWELL; 3. ANDRE CRENSHAW; 4. DON REYNOLDS; 5. BOBBY MOORE; 6. TONY CHERRY; 7. JONATHAN STEWART; 8. MEL RENFRO; 9. KENJON BARNER; 10. ANDIEL BROWN.

Dick James Sudoku (from page 51)

I	C	D	S	K	J	M	E	A
S	K	E	M	I	A	D	J	C
A	M	J	C	E	D	K	S	I
J	A	C	K	M	E	S	I	D
D	S	M	A	J	I	C	K	E
K	E	I	D	C	S	A	M	J
E	D	A	I	S	M	J	C	K
M	J	K	E	A	C	I	D	S
C	I	S	J	D	K	E	A	M

He Said What? (from page 50)

"I DON'T KNOW WHERE THEIR PITCH GUY COMES FROM. ONE TIME HE CAME FROM UNDERNEATH THE ASTROTURF AND SHOWED UP AS THE PITCH GUY."

Running Backs Crossword (from page 46)

Running Backs Word Search (from page 55)

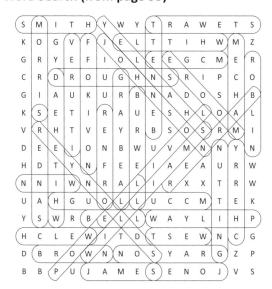

Running Backs Trivia (from page 52)

1. Bobby Moore.
2. LaMichael James (2010), Jonathan Stewart (2007), Saladin McCullough (1997), Bobby Moore (1971), Robert Sanders (1949), Jake Leicht (1947) and Curt Mecham (1941).

3. Dave Grayson (165 yards) and Cleveland Jones (107) at Utah.
4. Sean Burwell (153 yards) and Whittle (113) vs. Idaho in 1992, and Dino Philyaw (137) and Whittle (177) vs. Cal in 1994.
5. Tuffy Leeman.
6. Derek Loville (1986-89) and Sean Burwell (1990-93).
7. LaMichael James, 18 times, 2009 through the 2010 season.
8. Reuben Droughns, in 1998.
9. Onterrio Smith, at Washington State in 2001.
10. Jonathan Stewart.
11. Jack Morris, 212 yards (in just 15 carries) at USC in 1957.
12. Terrence Whitehead (2002-05), Ricky Whittle (1992-95), Sean Burwell (1990-93) and Derek Loville (1986-89).
13. Gary Beck, with 131 yards vs. Oregon State in 1977.
14. Toby Gerhart, 223 yards at Stanford in 2009.
15. Reuben Droughns, vs. Arizona.
16. 10.
17. Maurice Morris, 2,415 yards in 2000-01.
18. Derek Loville, 41 from 1986-89.
19. Sean Burwell, who had 969 rushing yards in 1990 as a freshman.
20. LeGarrette Blount.
21. Jeremiah Johnson, from 2005-08.
22. Don Reynolds.
23. Tony Cherry.
24. Reuben Droughns.
25. Saladin McCullough.

Chapter 5

Barnes Sudoku (from page 62)

A	S	N	R	E	B
R	E	B	A	S	N
N	A	S	B	R	E
B	R	E	S	N	A
E	B	R	N	A	S
S	N	A	E	B	R

Receivers Short Yardage (from page 56)

Additional Clue: OBEE

		H	O	W	R	Y	
O	R	I	G	I	N	A	T	E
F	O	R	E	N	A	M	E	S
T	W	E	E	N		S	A	P
			S	E	T		
P	R	O		B	E	R	E	T
S	U	L	T	A	N	A	T	E
I	N	D	I	G	E	N	C	E
			S	C	O	T	T	

Paysinger Sudoku (from page 58)

R	I	E	S	Y	N	P	A	G
N	G	Y	A	P	I	S	E	R
A	P	S	R	E	G	N	Y	I
P	S	A	G	N	Y	I	R	E
G	E	N	I	A	R	Y	S	P
Y	R	I	P	S	E	A	G	N
I	A	P	E	R	S	G	N	Y
S	Y	R	N	G	P	E	I	A
E	N	G	Y	I	A	R	P	S

Offsides Sudoku (from page 59)

G	I	P	N	E	A	R	S	Y
N	R	E	S	P	Y	G	I	A
S	Y	I	G	A	E	P	R	N
A	E	G	I	N	S	Y	P	R
E	P	N	Y	R	G	S	A	I
I	A	S	R	Y	P	E	N	G
R	N	Y	P	S	I	A	G	E
P	G	A	E	I	R	N	Y	S
Y	S	R	A	G	N	I	E	P

Dynamic Duos (from page 62)

2009 MAEHL, DICKSON; 2005 WILLIAMS, FINLEY; 2001 HOWRY, WILLIS; 1997 JOHNSON, SPENCE; 1993 TATE, DEADWILER; 1989 HARGAIN, REITZUG; 1985 DEBISSCHOP, BARNES; 1981 MOSER, HOGENSEN; 1977 VINCENT, PAGE; 1973 PALM, FRANCIS.

Building Blocks (from page 67)

1. O; 2. OR; 3. ORE; 4. GORE; 5. OGRES; 6. ROGERS.

Change Ups (from page 67)

1.TERRY OBEE; 2. LEW BARNES; 3. GREG MOSER; 4. RICKY WARD; 5. KEN PAGE; 6. BOB PALM; 7. SAMIE PARKER; 8. BOBBY MOORE.

Receivers Crossword (from page 60)

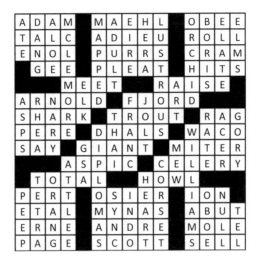

Receivers Word Search (from page 63)

Receivers Trivia (from page 64)

1. Russ Francis, who missed an entire UO season with a broken leg.
2. Bob Newland, who had 125 career receptions.
3. Bob Newland, with 67 catches in 1970.
4. Ahmad Rashad (Bobby Moore), who made his one shot.
5. Samie Parker, vs. Minnesota in the Sun Bowl.
6. Tony Hartley, vs. Washington.
7. Lew Barnes, who had 2,048 yards from 1983-85.

8. Keenan Howry, vs. Arizona State in 2001.
9. Jaison Williams (174 from 2005-08), Demetrius Williams (162 from 2002-05), Bobby Moore (131 from 1969-71), Ed Dickson (124 from 2006-09) and Terry Obee (122 from 1986-89).
10. Samie Parker in 2003 and Jeff Maehl in 2010.
11. Bob Newland, in 1970.
12. Terry Obee, 1987-89.
13. Sept. 22, 2007, by Cameron Colvin (136 yards) and Jaison Williams (113).
14. 2003—Keenan Howry, 2004—Samie Parker, 2005—Marcus Maxwell, 2006—Demetrius Williams, 2007—Jordan Kent.
15. George "Tarzan" Christensen, who played for the Portsmouth Spartans and Detroit Lions.
16. Raymond "Butch" Morse.
17. Lew Barnes, who had 93 punt returns and nine kickoff returns in the NFL, including an 85-yard KOR for a touchdown in his rookie season.
18. Demetrius Williams, whose best NFL season was 22 catches for 396 yards and two TDs as a rookie in 2006.
19. Matt Larkin.
20. Keenan Howry, in 2001.
21. Justin Peelle.
22. Kevin Howry, who made a sliding catch in the end zone for a game-winning TD in the 1999 Sun Bowl.
23. Samie Parker.
24. Bobby DeBisschop.
25. Cristin McLemore.

Chapter 6

Offensive Line Trivia (from page 76)

1. Steve Barnett.
2. Tom Drougas.
3. Max Unger.
4. Gary Zimmerman.
5. Gary Zimmerman.
6. Ed Moshofsky was a lineman for the Ducks from 1939-42 who made a fortune in the lumber business. The team's indoor practice facility also bears his name as thank you for a large donation.
7. Center Max Unger, from 2006-08.
8. Center Dave Tobey.
9. Eric Barnes. His daughter, Erica, was a freshman at U of A in 2010-11.
10. Steve Hardin, who was quoted in *Sports Illustrated* explaining why the UO students were fair-weather football fans: "Too many hippies."
11. 1997—Paul Wiggins, 2005—Adam Snyder.
12. Brad Ecklund.

13. Seaton Daly.
14. Stefan deVries.
15. Enoka Lucas (2003-06), Geoff Schwartz (2004-07), Adam Snyder (2001-04), Max Unger (2005-08) and Dan Weaver (2000-03).
16. Steve Greatwood, who has the title of Running Game Coordinator.
17. Dan Weaver.
18. Robin Knebel.
19. Honolulu, Hawaii.
20. Bo Thran.
21. Ryan Schmid.
22. Fenuki Tupou, who was drafted by the Philadelphia Eagles in the fifth round.
23. Geoff Schwartz.
24. Curt Dykes.
25. Center William Mayther in 1944 and '45.

Snyder Sudoku (from page 71)

Y	N	R	D	E	S
E	D	S	N	Y	R
S	E	N	R	D	Y
D	R	Y	S	N	E
N	S	E	Y	R	D
R	Y	D	E	S	N

Offensive Line Short Yardage (from page 68)

Additional Clue: ADAMS

P	A	D			M	O	E	N
A	G	E		L	A	U	R	A
L	A	C		E	N	T	R	Y
	T	O	W	I	T			
	E	R	A		R	I	G	
		Y	E	A	R	N		
S	M	E	L	L		A	A	H
A	B	E	A	M		T	W	O
D	A	L	Y			E	S	T

Six Down Linemen (from page 79)

T	C	L	E	A	S
S	T	E	C	L	A
L	A	S	T	C	E
E	L	T	A	S	C
A	E	C	S	T	L
C	S	A	L	E	T

O-Line Word Search (from page 70)

Floyd Rhea Sudoku (from page 71)

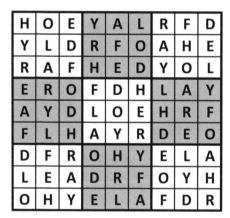

Double Switch (from page 80)

1. NICK STEITZ; 2. MAX UNGER; 3. TOM DROUGAS; 4. STEVE BARNETT; 5. RYAN SCHMID; 6. CARSON YORK; 7. ENOKA LUCAS; 8. DAVE WILCOX; 9. JIM ADAMS; 10. DEKE MOEN.

Ducks Fill-in (from page 81)

C.E. KAISER

O-Line Name Grid (from page 72)

Offensive Linemen Crossword (from page 74)

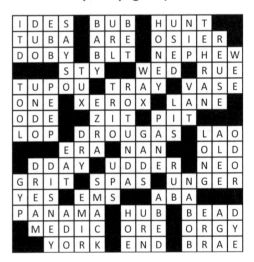

Chapter 7

BYRD Combos (from page 84)

The missing combinations are BRYD, DYBR and RBYD.

Build the Name (from page 88)

1. PHINISEE; 2. FLETCHER; 3. WHEATON; 4. BRANTLEY; 5. GOLDSMITH; 6. COLEMAN;
7. HILDRETH; 8. PHILLIPS; 9. MORETTI; 10. BANDISON.

Mikels Sudoku (from page 88)

M	I	K	S	L	E
S	L	E	M	I	K
E	K	L	I	S	M
I	S	M	E	K	L
K	M	I	L	E	S
L	E	S	K	M	I

Defenders Short Yardage (from page 82)

Additional Clue: FARWELL

B	L	O	C		M	E	H	L
R	E	D	O		O	R	E	O
A	D	E	N		I	A	M	B
			C	O	S	T	A	
	W	H	E	A	T	O	N	
	H	A	I	K	U			
F	I	S	T		R	E	N	D
A	N	T	E		E	V	E	N
R	E	E	D		S	E	T	A

Who Am I? Sudoku (from page 84)

Vince GOLDSMITH

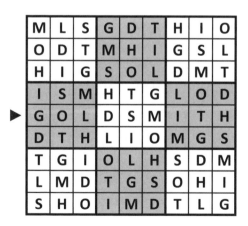

Defenders Trivia (from page 89)

1. Mario Clark.
2. Vince Goldsmith, who put the shot at UO and ranks sixth in school history.
3. John Kitzmiller, who played for Oregon from 1927-30.
4. Alex Molden.

5. Haloti Ngata.
6. Nick Reed.
7. Mel Renfro.
8. George Shaw, who had a school record 13 interceptions in 1951.
9. Jim Smith, who grew up in Yazoo City, Miss.
10. Kenny Wheaton.
11. Dave Wilcox.
12. Chad Cota, who had an eight-year NFL career with the Panthers, Saints, Colts and Rams.
13. Herman O'Berry.
14. Chris Oldham.
15. Steve Smith, vs. Colorado in 2002. He also had three interceptions vs. USC in 2001.
16. Tom Graham.
17. Nick Reed (2008) and Ernest Jones (1993).
18. Patrick Chung, with 384 from 2005-08.
19. Saul Patu, with 53 from 1997-2000.
20. Alex Molden, with 60 from 1992-95.
21. Jairus Byrd, with 17 from 2006-08.
22. Joe Farwell, from 1990-92.
23. Linebacker Wesley Mallard, with 111 tackles.
24. Yazoo Smith.
25. Dave Moretti.

Defensive Players Word Search (from page 85)

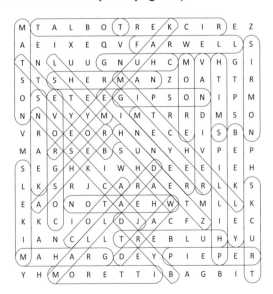

Defenders Crossword (from page 86)

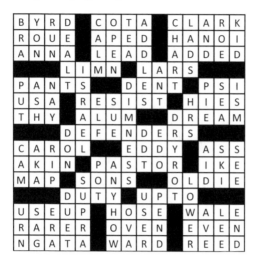

Chapter 8

Oldham Sudoku (from page 98)

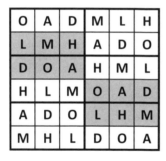

Special Teams Short Yardage (from page 92)

Additional Clue: CLEATS

		A	K	A		H	A	Y
C	H	U	N	G		E	L	M
A	U	G	E	R		D	E	C
T	H	U	L	E		G	S	A
		S	T	E	L	E		
E	A	T		A	O	R	T	A
S	K	I		B	R	O	A	D
S	I	N		L	E	W	I	S
E	N	E		E	N	S		

Special Teams Trivia (from page 99)

1. Jonathan Stewart, who averaged 33.7 yards per return.
2. Josh Frankel, who made a 27-yarder. "The feeling after that was truly special, almost a Rudy-like scene," said Frankel, now a financial advisor in Portland.
3. Kenjon Barner, a 100-yarder at UCLA.
4. Haloti Ngata, who blocked three field goal attempts, three extra point attempts and one punt.
5. Keenan Howry, vs. Stanford.
6. Jared Siegel, at UCLA in 2002.
7. Gregg McCallum, with 24 in 1989.
8. Matt MacLeod, in 1985.
9. Josh Bidwell.
10. Nathan Villegas, .825 (33-for-40) in 1998-99.
11. Mike Preacher, 42.9 yards per punt from 1984-86.
12. Walter Thurmond III, with 15.0 yards per return from 2006-09.
13. Woodley Lewis, with 34.1 yards per return from 1948-49.
14. Josh Syria.
15. Kenjon Barner.
16. Morgan Flint, who was 82-for-82 from 2006-09.
17. Six.
18. 15.
19. Oct. 24, 2009, at Washington. Rory Cavaille blocked the punt; Tyrell Irvin fell on the ball for a TD.
20. 75 yards, at Michigan State in 1999.
21. True freshman Drew Howell.
22. Backup quarterback Nate Costa.
23. Matt Belden, in 1994.
24. Tom Blanchard.
25. Josh Bidwell, who punted for the Ducks from 1995-98.

Special Teams Crossword (from page 94)

H	I	C	K	S		P	A	L	M		T	O	P	S
A	D	I	E	U		A	L	O	E		U	G	L	I
M	O	D	E	M		Y	E	G	G		C	L	U	E
			N	A	T	O		A	S	K	I	N	G	
I	N	S		C	E	L	E	B		T	I	N	G	E
T	O	A	D		L	A	V	A		A	N	G	E	L
S	E	R	U	M			E	L	A	N				
	L	I	E	U		A	N	D		C	O	M	A	
			E	L	L	S			E	L	E	C	T	
A	R	I	E	S		M	E	L	T		D	O	M	E
R	E	N	A	L		S	N	O	O	P		W	E	E
R	U	S	S	I	A			C	O	L	A			
O	B	O	E		T	H	R	U		U	P	E	N	D
Y	E	L	L		O	R	E	S		M	E	D	E	A
O	N	E	S		P	S	S	T		B	R	O	W	N

Fill the Grid (from page 96)

L	Y	E
E	E	K
A	W	E

O	U	Z	O
S	T	I	R
L	A	T	E
O	H	I	O

Special Teams Word Search (from page 97)

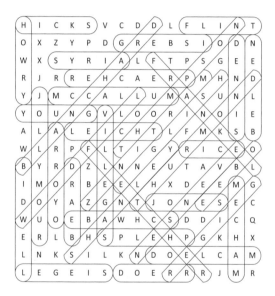

Showalter Sudoku (from page 98)

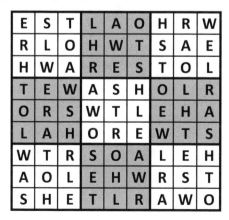

E	S	T	L	A	O	H	R	W
R	L	O	H	W	T	S	A	E
H	W	A	R	E	S	T	O	L
T	E	W	A	S	H	O	L	R
O	R	S	W	T	L	E	H	A
L	A	H	O	R	E	W	T	S
W	T	R	S	O	A	L	E	H
A	O	L	E	H	W	R	S	T
S	H	E	T	L	R	A	W	O

Chapter 9

Who Am I? Sudoku (from page 110)

Tex OLIVER

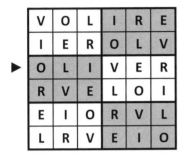

Coaches Short Yardage (from page 102)

Additional Clue: CAREER

	R	E	A	D		L	A	O
	E	C	R	U		E	L	F
O	P	T	E	D		F	I	T
P	R	O	T	E	C	T		
P	O	M	E		R	A	T	E
	O	S	C	U	L	A	R	
A	P	R		A	D	O	R	E
G	A	P		L	E	N	S	
A	S	H		F	R	E	I	

Coaches Crossword (from page 106)

S	C	O	T		A	L	E	E		A	B	E	D
H	A	L	O		L	E	F	T	Y		L	E	G	O
A	L	I	T		L	A	T	H	E		S	L	O	E
R	I	V	A	L			S	Y	M	B	O	L	
O	C	E	L	O	T		L	E	E		O	D	D
N	O	R		B	O	O	B		N	E	C	T	A	R
		F	O	N	D	U		R	A	T	I	O
F	O	C	I		K	E	L	L	Y		L	I	S	P
I	N	A	N	E		G	O	O	F	F	
R	I	S	E	U	P		E	T	U	I		B	E	D
E	T	A		R	A	G		S	T	A	R	V	E
	N	O	O	D	L	E		S	C	O	O	T
O	D	O	R		R	A	L	L	Y		T	O	K	E
N	O	V	A		E	R	A	S	E		U	K	E	S
E	T	A	L		E	N	D	S		P	S	S	T

Wordsmith Challenge (from page 105)

CEIL, CELL, CELLI, CHIEL, CHILE, CHILL, CHILLY, CHIP, CHYLE, CLIP, CLYPEI, ELHI, EPIC, HECK, HEIL, HELL, HELP, HICK, HICKEY, HIKE, HILL, HILLY, HIPLY, HYPE, ICKY, ILLY, KELLY, KELP, KELPY, KEPI, KILL, LECH, LICE, LICH, LICK, LIKE, LIKELY, LILY, LIPE, LYCH, PECH, PECK, PECKY, PHYLE, PHYLIC, PICE, PICK, PICKLE, PICKY, PIKE, PILE, PILL, PILY, PLIE, PYIC, YECH, YELK, YELL, YELP, YILL, YIPE.

Coaching Boxes (from page 104)

		S	H	O	R	T	S	
		E	N	R	I	G	H	T
		F	R	E	I			
	Y	O	U	N	G			
		B	R	O	O	K	S	
	A	I	K	E	N			
	S	M	I	T	H			
	O	L	I	V	E	R		
		S	P	E	A	R	S	
				D	O	L	P	H
			M	C	E	W	A	N
	B	E	L	L	O	T	T	I
			R	E	A	D		
		F	R	I	C	K		
			C	H	U	R	C	H
			K	E	L	L	Y	
		F	R	O	S	T		

Coaches Word Search (from page 109)

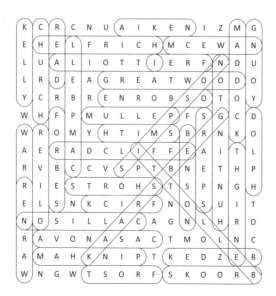

155

Cryptic Quote (from page 108)

"WE HAVE AN ATTACK MINDSET FROM THE GET-GO. WE'RE GOING TO TRY TO PRESSURE YOU IN AS MANY WAYS AS WE CAN, FROM THE TEMPO WE PLAY AT TO THE FORMATIONS WE RUN."

John McKay Sudoku (from page 110)

A	J	M	H	N	C	O	K	Y
K	O	C	J	Y	A	N	M	H
H	N	Y	M	K	O	J	A	C
M	A	N	K	C	H	Y	J	O
C	Y	K	N	O	J	M	H	A
O	H	J	Y	A	M	K	C	N
Y	C	O	A	M	K	H	N	J
J	M	A	O	H	N	C	Y	K
N	K	H	C	J	Y	A	O	M

Coaches Trivia (from page 111)

1. Shy Huntington, who played for Oregon in the 1917 Rose Bowl and coached Oregon in the 1920 Rose Bowl.
2. California State University, Chico. He was 21-25-2 from 1984-88, then left to become the offensive coordinator at Oregon.
3. Mike Bellotti, whose Ducks were 11-1 in 2001.
4. Rich Brooks.
5. St. Louis Rams; he was 13-19 in 1995-96.
6. Oregon State, where he was a defensive back and graduated in 1963.
7. Portland State, from 1968-71 and 1981-85.
8. Dick Enright.
9. Jerry Frei.
10. Jerry Frei. He refused to fire his staff and resigned.
11. Len Casanova.
12. Len Casanova.
13. Jim Aiken.
14. Tex Oliver, who was 23-28-3 over six seasons.
15. Prink Callison, who was 33-23-2 with Oregon from 1932-37.
16. Hugo Bezdek.
17. John McEwan, who was 20-13-2 at Oregon from 1926-29.
18. John Warren, whose name is on UO's basketball team's Most Inspirational Player Award.
19. C.W. Spears. During his tenure, the Oregon team was known as the Spearsmen.
20. Dr. Clarence Wiley (C.W.) "Doc" Spears, who studied medicine at the University of Chicago and Rush Medical College during his coaching career and then maintained a medical practice until he died at age 69.

Chip Kelly Trivia (from page 113)

1. Oregon 38, Purdue 36, in 2009.
2. Stanford, in 2009.
3. University of New Hampshire, Class of 1990.
4. Columbia University, as the freshman secondary and special teams coach.
5. Football (starting QB), ice hockey and track (team captain).

Chapter 10

Autzen Sudoku (from page 117)

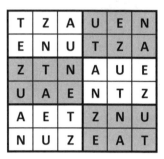

Overtime Short Yardage (from page 114)

Additional Clue: SIMPSON

S	N	U	B	N	O	S	E	D
W	A	S				O	N	E
O	N		S	U	P		D	O
R		A	P	N	E	A		D
D		D	U	C	K	S		O
F		O	R	L	O	P		R
I	S		T	E	E		M	A
S	O	U				W	I	N
H	Y	P	E	R	T	E	X	T

Presidential Box (from page 116)

AERIE, AERIER, AID, AIR, AIRER, AIRIER, ARC, ARCH, ARE, AREA, ARIA, ARID, ARIL, ARREAR, ARRIVE, ARRIVER, CIRRI, CRIER, DIE, DIRE, DIRER, DIVE, DIVER, DREAR, DREARIER, DRIER, DRIVE, DRIVER, EAR, ERA, ERE, ERR, ERVIL, EVIL, ICH, IRE, IRIDIC, LID, LIE, LIER, LIRA, LIRE, LIVE, LIVER, LIVRE, RAID, RARE, RARER, REAR, REI, REIVE, REIVER, REV, RICH, RID, RIVE, RIVER, VEIL, VERIDIC, VERIER, VIE, VIER, VIRID.

Missing D-U-C-K (from page 117)

1, TRUCKED; 2. CHUCKED; 3. SUNDECK; 4. BUCKLED; 5. DUCKPIN; 6. QUACKED; 7. MUDPACK; 8. CAULKED.

Quote Pickup (from page 120)

"SOME SPORTS CARS LOOK FAST WHILE PARKED. AUTZEN SOUNDS LOUD WHILE EMPTY."

Overtime Crossword (from page 118)

S	A	S	S		C	A	B	L	E		D	A	R	E
P	L	O	Y		I	N	L	A	Y		I	B	I	S
E	O	N	S		A	T	O	N	E		V	A	M	P
W	H	A	T	D	O	I	C	A	L	L	A			
S	A	R	E	E			I	I	I		F	E	D	
		M	A	L	T	A		D	E	S	I	R	E	
A	A	H		L	E	A	V	E		A	X	I	S	
S	M	A	R	T	O	R	E	G	O	N	D	U	C	K
T	E	R	N		P	R	O	V	O		P	A	S	
I	B	E	A	M	S		T	S	A	R	S			
R	A	M		E	M	U			M	O	O	S	E	
		A	W	I	S	E	Q	U	A	C	K	E	R	
N	U	M	B		T	U	T	U	S		C	A	R	E
E	T	A	L		E	R	N	I	E		E	P	I	C
D	E	N	Y		S	P	A	T	S		R	I	F	T

One and Only One (from page 121)

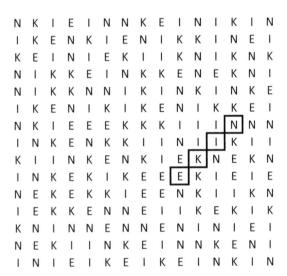

Ducks TXT (from page 123)

1. MAEHL; 2. DAVIS; 3. PLEASANT; 4. HOLMES; 5. PAYSINGER; 6. JACKSON; 7. BAIR;
8. ROWE; 9. BARNER; 10. LEWIS.

Across & Down Words (from page 124)

Across: 1. RUSH; 2. PLAY; 3. ENDS; 4. PUNT; 5. BALL; 6. FLAG; 7. PASS.
Down: 1. TACKLED; 2. QUARTER; 3. DEFENSE; 4. KICKOFF. Hidden Phrase: EUGENE,
OREGON IS HOME TO THE DUCKS.

Quote Box (from page 125)

"PER SQUARE YARD, IT'S THE LOUDEST STADIUM IN THE HISTORY OF THE PLANET."

32	31	30	29	28	27	26
33	36	37	38	39	40	25
34	35	56	55	54	41	24
3	2	1	52	53	42	23
4	11	12	51	50	43	22
5	10	13	48	49	44	21
6	9	14	47	46	45	20
7	8	15	16	17	18	19

Fourth Down (from page 125)

PIONEER. The other four words contain the names of UO players who won the
Skeie's Award, given annually to the team's outstanding player.
bREEDer, midWESTern, pLUNGer, raspBERRY.

Stefanick Sudoku (From page 129)

E	C	F	S	I	K	A	T	N
A	T	S	F	N	E	C	K	I
I	K	N	C	A	T	E	F	S
N	E	A	T	C	I	F	S	K
F	I	K	N	E	S	T	C	A
C	S	T	A	K	F	I	N	E
S	N	C	E	T	A	K	I	F
K	F	E	I	S	C	N	A	T
T	A	I	K	F	N	S	E	C

Overtime Trivia (from page 126)

1. J.W. Beckett.
2. Dan Fouts, with Al Michaels and Dennis Miller, in 2000 and '01.
3. Dan Fouts, who played an ESPN announcer with Brent Musberger.
4. Bobby Moore, as a wide receiver in 1969 and as a running back in '70.
5. Nick Reed (2008) and Steve Barnett (1962).
6. Mel Renfro.
7. George Shaw, who was an All-American in both football and baseball.
8. Jim Shanley.
9. Kenny Wheaton, who played three seasons with the Dallas Cowboys.
10. Fred Quillan, an offensive lineman who lettered for the Ducks from 1975-77 and later played in two Super Bowls.
11. Mario Clark, Russ Francis, Fred Quillan, Jeff Stover and Mike Walter.
12. Mike Jorgensen, who was the UO starter in 1982 and '83.
13. Top Performer on Special Teams.
14. Ohio State.
15. Portland lumberman, sportsman and philanthropist, Thomas J. Autzen.
16. Longtime Oregon Head Coach Rich Brooks.
17. Michigan Stadium.
18. Rueben Mayes, in 1984.
19. University of Kentucky.
20. Jerry Allen.
21. Portland seven times (most recently in 1952) and Albany twice (in 1912 and '13).
22. Platypus Trophy.
23. "Oregon Classic" and "State Championship Game."
24. Oregon State, 23-13, at Corvallis.
25. Stanford and Cal, in the "Big Game."